The In-Between Gang

Leona Nicholas Welch

THE IN-BETWEEN GANG

Leona Nicholas Welch

Reprinted 2019

PUBLISHED BY:
BRENTWOOD PUBLISHERS GROUP
POST OFFICE BOX 4773
COLUMBUS, GEORGIA 31914-4773
(800) 334-8861
WWW.BRENTWOODBOOKS.COM

Dedication

I dedicate this book to my children: James, Jr., Bridget, Derrick Sr., JaMar, Mishanne, and Kyra, and to my grand-children: Raina, Derrick, Jr., Trevor, Sadara, DaWud, Caimar, Inara, Christian, and Anthony. Thank you all for your love!

Acknowledgements

In the course of writing THE IN-BETWEEN GANG, I have relied upon and consulted with the young and the mature reader. Each, in her or his own way, has contributed to the completion of the book. I thank the following:

Calitha L. Chaney
DaWud J. Coleman
Mary Jo Johnson
Jamere S. Sneed
Jamia P. Sneed
Bridget M. Welch
Derrick C. Welch
JaMar N. Welch
Rosalind J. Welch

Preface

The In-Between Gang

PURPOSE FOR THE BOOK: There are gangs, and we all know it. We worry about them. We pray about them. We talk about them, and we work to prevent and to end them, and to rehabilitate the young people involved in them.

There are high achieving youth. They work hard and they study diligently. They frequently approach the podium to receive deserving awards, and then they go on to do great things. Of these we are immensely proud, as well we should be. We hug them, encourage them, give them generous allowances, and apply all bragging rights.

There is a third category of youth, not forgotten, and not remembered. The truth is, we hardly know that they exist. These are not hard-core gang members. These youth have never fired a gun or taken a life on the streets. They are not bad kids, but no one would point them out for commendations. These have most likely not robbed a Seven-Eleven; yet, they live precariously on the edge of society, for they seek for something "more." These youth are not making it in school or at home, so they huddle together in constant search for a place to belong. I call them the "in-betweens." They could be helped, if only someone would notice.

It is around this latter group of youth and young adults that I have weaved my story, *The In-Between Gang.* Set in contemporary Oakland, California, this book is intended to bring attention to a potentially endangered group of young people. Besides being a good read, *The In-Between Gang* is a call for help for some who cannot call for themselves.

This book is highly and urgently recommended for schools and youth groups in all areas of life, and would be a tool of empowerment in the hands of adults who are working to make a positive change in the lives of young people. A compelling, yet a quick and comfortable read, *The In-Between Gang* is conducive to discussions and open forums on issues that plague our youth. An eye-opener and a heart-opener, this book was written to help.

Chapter One

A Sad Reminder

This I don't need

"One year. One whole year. It's been one year already," Bull murmured as he recalled his visit to Rolling Hills Cemetery earlier that day. It was now around eight at night that same Friday, and he had not been able to shake the heavy sadness engulfing him. He still found it hard to believe that his brother was gone. It had taken all the strength he had to bring himself to go to the cemetery. He and Jay were close, and that horrible night still held Bull in its bloody grip. It was as present with him today as it was when he stood trembling, locked in total disbelief at his brother dying from a gunshot wound in front of a Seven Eleven.

"He wasn't suppose to die. It wasn't suppose to go down like this." Bull could hear his own voice screaming inside of his head. "Jay!"

Kebo, they called him on the streets. But to Bull, he would always be Jay, the brother he knew better than any gang member could ever know. Not one of them could imagine the childhood memories with a middle brother who always had his back, even if it meant taking Bull's punishment because it hurt Jay to see his little brother in trouble. Bull knew how they would sneer at him if he told them that his brother needed hugs and kind words, just as he frequently gave both.

The hard, hot knots burned in Bull's guts at the thought – the first anniversary of Jay's death, and no one had been convicted of the shooting. In fact, Bull believed that the cops had closed the case without even telling the family.

"They just don't care. Brothers dying left and right, right here in Oakland, and all over the Bay, and nobody can find out a thing." He took in a deep, exasperating breath and blew it out. Absent-mindedly, Bull wiped the stinging tears from his eyes and stepped outside his apartment building, and onto the street. He began to walk the distance up Fruitvale Avenue, from his place at Lynde, to Elbow's on School Street.

He paused in front of the dull gray apartment building he shared with his older brother, Hal. Taking in the sights across the street, he noted that his end of Fruitvale was coming alive, taking on its usual Friday night face. The weekend people traffic created an endless buzz and flow, unlike any other night. The Fortune Cookie Chinese Restaurant, where he sometimes sat and enjoyed a heaping plate of chicken Chow Mein and three or four shrimp and vegetable egg rolls, was popping with pre-party hoppers, filling up on a "lil Su'm Su'm." before hittin' the scene.

Shifting his attention, Bull caught sight of three young black women in their mid-twenties as they hopped out of a parked black Altima and rushed into *New's Hair and Nails Shop*, two doors to the right of the restaurant. No doubt, they were in a hurry for a beauty hook-up before their big night.

Late evening smells hit his nostrils like a sudden gush of water from a front-yard hose. Bull was overwhelmed by the smell of greasy, pungent foods from the restaurant and the hot oils and chemicals that wafted from the beauty shop.

He stood there, his pain tugging at his mind. He stared back at his apartment, tempted to go back inside. Shaking his head, determinedly, he turned and focused his attention again on the opposite side of the street. He observed two teenage boys, one Latino, and the other black, slip into Fruitvale Liquors, that sat between The *Fortune Cookie* and *New's Hair*. He could see the two just inside the liquor store, bringing themselves up to full height, shoulders back, feigning maturity. For sure, they hoped that tonight the old man wouldn't toss them out before they had purchased their favorite wine cooler.

Letting his eyes take in the entire corner, Bull focused for a moment on an elderly Chinese woman, lean and bent, carrying an oversized shopping bag decorated in bright orange, pink and green Chinese calligraphy. It appeared that everybody was focused on the best way to spend this night, but him.

The unsettled feeling, the sadness that had held him all day, since he'd left the cemetery, wouldn't let go of its grip. If not for Elbow, he would forget the homeboys tonight. He would put everybody and everything out of his head. But Elbow would be waiting. It was Elbow who had proudly assured the others that while he kept watch at one end of Fruitvale, Bull had their backs at the other end. No, he wouldn't let his partna down.

Slowly he picked up one foot, then the other, and in just a few minutes his body had locked into the pattern of his long, easy stride, and before he knew it, he was swiftly making his way block after block, to Elbow's and the trouble waiting at the place they all called The Home. Deliberately, he allowed the balmy spring night air to drift through his mind in an attempt to free himself of the tension that threatened him.

"Troubleshootin' time at The Home," he sighed as he walked. The Homeboys were restless, and no matter how he felt today, this matter had to be settled. With this thought racing through his head, Bull picked up his pace even more.

"Hey Bull! Bull, man. Wait up!"

Bull looked back to see Mack waving him down and slow-jogging up the middle of Fruitvale, crossing the street to catch up with him. As though he didn't have enough on his mind already, Bull would have to run into somebody demanding his attention. With thoughts of Jay, worries about his family, and all the stress and upheaval going on with the homeboys over at Elbow's crib, he did not need this intrusion from Mack, of all people. Mack was a thorn in Bull's side. The only thing he ever had on his mind was getting high and working some sort of scheme.

Mack was a gang banging wanna-be. Because of the way he liked to hang around with Bull, the Whips, Bull's old gang, had let Mack hang around them too; but no one took him seriously. He was no threat to anyone, and sometimes he even came in handy to run an errand or stand watch when "Su'm was up."

Bull could not explain it, but he always felt uneasy around Mack. There was something about him that just rubbed Bull the wrong way. Part of it had to do with the way Mack would side with one member of the Whips one minute and switch sides the next, depending on who had hooked him up with some weed or some malt liquor or a wine cooler. Every time he saw Mack he did everything he could not to have to talk to him. Today he was caught.

"Hey, Bull, wait up." Mack forced his short, stocky body into a slow trot toward Bull. "Bull! Hey dude, don't make a brutha sweat. Hold up dude."

"This I don't need," Bull thought. So much for clearing his head before meeting with the brothers. He wished he had seen Mack before Mack saw him. Turning abruptly, he stopped in the middle of the sidewalk and positioned himself to face his trailer.

"Hey, Mack, what's crackin'?" Bull tried not to let his disgust show. The sight of Mack always took him back to his street life and the trouble he had left behind. Mack reminded him too vividly of the Whips, and thoughts of the Whips always took him back to that horrible night. Once again he could hear the sirens wailing in that dark, wet street the night Jay died.

Bull had to fight off the urge to walk away, leaving Mack standing there with his clenched fist extended in the air waiting for him to give him a dap. It had been several months since he had last seen Mack, and he was in no mood right now to be kind to someone he'd rather not look at.

"You act like you don't wanna see a brutha playa', Mack said, grinning, still waiting for Bull to return his greeting.

"Just in a hurry," Bull answered, knocking his clenched fist against Mack's.

Again, the picture began to form in Bull's mind. He could see Jay on the cold, wet concrete, doubled up in his own blood in front of that store. The red lights of the ambulance circled in Bull's head as the picture became much too clear.

"Where you been hidin', Bull? Nobody knows where you be these days. Just dropped us like we all hot. Is that any way to treat a homie"?

"I been 'round," Bull mumbled.

"Couldn't prove it by me," Mack laughed. "It's still goin' down, dude. Just say the word. Boxer always said – anytime you want back, all you got to do is say the word. Know what I'm sayin' bruh?"

"I'm cool. Into some other stuff. I ain't trippin'."

"Yeah, well, you know me." Mack grinned again. "Always lookin' out for a homie. You change your mind, hit me up," he said, taking his iPhone from his shirt pocket and placing it back, all in a breath.

Bull saw Mack standing in front of him, and he heard Mack's voice droning on like it was somewhere far in a distant open field. Yet his mind continued to race back to the conclusion of that night, just two years following the death of their father to cancer. In his mind, he could see the deep blue of the police uniforms, the glittering of guns under the light of a full moon as police barricaded the area around Jay's body. There must have been a dozen black and white patrol cars parked around the area. Bull could see the yellow tape that separated his brother's body from the people standing around gawking.

He had arrived on the scene just after the shooting. Earlier, he had been given word by Boxer, the leader of the Whips, that something was "goin' down." As Bull stood there caught up in his thoughts, Mack's face became a blur and his voice even more distant. Bull was lost in the memory.

"NO!" He had screamed into the night. "NO!" If only he'd been there. If only he'd moved faster. He had sprinted like crazy through the yellow tape and dropped to his knees, draping himself over his brother's bleeding body, weeping loudly and uncontrollably. A police officer had lifted him to his feet, led him aside, and waited for him to regain composure before asking him questions. His brother's blood on his hands, cheek and his new gray and white Polo, Bull had slumped against the patrol car and onto the ground.

"And Mama...." Bull let the thoughts take over. He did not hear the persistent droning of Mack's voice as he strode alongside Bull.

"That was the night we lost her," he thought. Jay and Mama, both in one night. Jay, to a bullet and Mama to the horror of it all. Poor Mama! Even now she's still trapped inside the pain in her mind. His mother had suffered a mental breakdown. The shock of Jay's death was just too much for her to handle. He could see it all so clearly again, as his pace picked up to accommodate the swiftness and the heaviness of his thoughts.

"You with me, man?" Mack's voice broke through Bull's painful reverie, making him even more disgusted that Mack was there. But the memories would not shut off. Like a faucet with a broken washer, images of that frightful night gushed in on him.

"He's gone. Jay's gone." His voice had been low and sad when he took the news home to his mother.

"Gone?" His mother had whispered. Your daddy's gone. Now Jay's gone. Don't you go, Sherman. Don't you go. Promise me you'll leave those gangs alone, Sherman. Promise."

Over the honking horns and the wail of a distant siren, over the loud clinking of the metal taps on the bottoms of his own shoes, hitting the pavement with a desperate rhythm, Bull could once again hear his own voice, answering his mother's plea as she desperately clung to him.

"I promise, Mama. I promise."

Bull had seen the dark cloud hovering around her face as his older brother, Hal, comforted their mother that night. He had seen it from the corner of the room where he had retreated, leaning with his back and head resting against the wall for support, still caught up in his own shock.

The cloud had washed over his mother's face like a shadow that crosses a wall in a dimly lit room. When the shadow had passed, his mother had been left sitting in a dark space. Her empty, brown eyes had told them that she too was gone. Her pain had engulfed her and drew her away from reality. In an hour Bull had been forced to say goodbye to two people he dearly loved.

"Bull! Mack's voice was loud and clear now."Come back dude. Whoa! Which end of town did you slip off to? man! and me here just flappin' my chops all over the place."

At the sound of Mack's voice, Bull shook his head to rid himself of his agonizing memories. There was Mack directly in front of him, walking backward, arms stretched wide, trying to get Bull's attention.

"Oh, yeah. Ah, yeah, Mack. Look Mack, I got to hurry. Got this errand to do for my brother. Check you later." With that Bull broke into a trot, ignoring Mack's call behind him. All he heard as he turned the corner onto Elbow's street was something from Mack about getting together sometime. Two blocks from Elbow's, Bull slowed his pace, shook him-

self again and adjusted his mind for what he was about to
face.

Chapter Two

CROSSROADS

Like bits of broken glass mixed with sand in a sandbox

When Bull arrived at Elbow's apartment, a brief ten minutes after his unwelcomed encounter with Mack, he found the place vacant. Bull let himself in with the key that Elbow had given him. "Hey man, if the leader can't be trusted, then who can?" Elbow had insisted when Bull attempted to refuse the key.

Grabbing himself a coke from the mini-fridge, Bull settled himself to wait. Taking his favorite posture against the wall, he slowly sipped the cold drink, allowing it to sooth his dry throat and his nerves. Running into Mack still had a hold on him, and he found himself glad for time alone. He could feel his thoughts closing in on him. Like bits of broken glass mixed with sand in a sandbox, Bull's thoughts grated on his mind, demanding his attention.

Bull stood there, his strong broad, six-foot, mahogany frame against the wall. His right foot rested flat on the floor, while he propped his left one on a red milk crate.

He'd heard of crossroads, but this was something else. His world, once so sure and set, so daring and fearless, was now split in several parts. He was caught off guard, and no one could help him. He, Bull Bullins, head man, sure-stepping as any horse on a mountain ridge; he, leader of The Home, felt his own footing uncertain and shaky lately. He was a young black man, in a large urban city, trying to make his way in spite of his drop-out status.

They called it "The Home." It was not the pad, the hide-out, the crib, or any other typical group-type name. They were not a gang, nor a club, nor anything easy to define. They were actually a group of misfits clinging to one another, trying to make a mark on life — crying for help. There were nine of them, each with a different failure story to tell. And Bull Bullins was expected to have all the answers for every one of them.

"Hey Bull, man, how come we don't see no action, man — huh?" Flippo's voice rang in his mind.

"Yeah, all we do is sit around here choppin' it up and let-tin' all the fun pass us by. I didn't leave my folks' house for this, Bull, man." Tailgate's voice had trailed close behind Flippo's.

A little over a year ago, they had gathered under the ban-ner of *Cause and Brotherhood*. They were all from the Oakland area, and all but one of them had dropped out of high school. Jake, the Space, an eighteen year old black, intellectual type, was so called by the others because of his love for books, especially poetry and Black history. Jake had managed to stagger out of continuation school on one foot and a diploma, after summer school. The others, including Bull, had left school at sixteen or seventeen. Their ages ranged from fourteen to twenty-one. Bull, himself, was nineteen.

All of the boys had families of one sort or another. Being a family on their own terms, they had among them an assort-ment of troubles. This Home was the only real hearth stone most of them really ever knew. Most people would call it ugly, but it was a family place to them.

The house that set back from the sidewalk, on School Street had burned on the outside at one corner of the build-ing. The cracked beige paint, what had not peeled off, had already turned dirty gray. The one bedroom house had once belonged to Sarge, an elderly black man who had retired from the army and used the money from his G-I Bill to put a modest roof over his head. Sarge had a heart for hard luck cases and had allowed Elbow to live with him temporarily. Sarge had died a year ago, and no one had bothered to claim the place yet, so Elbow was unofficially the proprietor. He had scratched up enough to pay the current taxes and called it home, until someone could prove otherwise.

The place wasn't much to look at, but it was a refuge. The undersized living room held a sunken gray-green couch, heavily stained with catsup, beer, and grease smears. This generously served as an extra bed, for anyone to "crash" at any time. Plastic red, blue and yellow milk crates lifted from the nearby school cafeteria, served as chairs. A stained gold and white remnant of linoleum, salvaged from the junk yard, covered the entire floor.

For some unexplained reason, the door between the tiny living room and Elbow's bedroom had been ripped down and replaced by a worn, tattered, green army blanket, tacked up by small nails. A sign that read "Elbow's Sanity Ward," written on a white poster board in large black letters was stapled to the make-shift curtain.

"Never had my own space, homies. You know I got y'all's back, but that's where I collect Elbow and keep him all together. Ya heard?" With this, he pointed to the room. It was clear to everyone that no one but Elbow was to cross that threshole, and no one has ever attempted.

Elbow's room was humbly furnished. A small lop-sided gray dresser sat to the left of a mattress on the floor. The mattress was covered with a well-worn, but clean quilt of orange brown and cream geometric designs. A pine-stained nightstand which held a small relic of a CD player and an 8x10 framed, colored photo of his entire family was positioned to the right of the mattress. A stack of dusty CD's was neatly tucked in a clear plastic box on the floor just beneath the stand.

Two sets of brown plastic drawers from the dollar store, were placed, one atop the other at the side of the closet, on the left side of the room. Elbow had talked a carpet dealer out of a piece of discarded brown carpet, on which his mattress set. The one new item in the entire place was the mattress, bought brand new from Costco.

"I never had a new mattress in my life," he had told the others, the one time he had shown them his room. "This is my one luxury. I crowned myself king when I saved to buy this baby." At this, he had squatted and gingerly patted the cheap mattress. Rising from the floor, he proudly scanned his room. Cheap, unattractive to others, maybe, but clean and orderly. This was Elbow's haven of peace.

While the bedroom was Elbow's, the living room, on the other hand, was everybody's. The boys had all contributed to the variety of posters that lined the faded, tan sheet-rocked wall around the room.

A 14x16, color photo of Tupac Shukur demanded a space in the center. Flippo had decided on memorializing the rap star by featuring him in the studio, "doin' his thing." The picture presented Tupac in a blue sleeveless tank, his neck adorned with a thick braided necklace and various other smaller pieces of neck jewelry. The star was wearing a studio headset, and his face wore a satisfied smile.

Snoop Dawgg was MopMan's contribution. Beyonce was presented by Elbow, himself. The "honey of the honeys," Elbow had laughed. Tailgate had brought in Christina Aguilera. "Me and Christina – Christina and me. Sweet!" And he'd kissed the image of the star on the lips, grinned and taped the 10x12, color picture on the wall, adjacent to the kitchen area.

There were several other smaller pictures posted randomly about the room. "Cinnamon, vanilla, and chocolate honeys," Bop called the black, Jet Magazine models he had placed on the right wall, as far from the others as he could.

18

He had taped the pictures in frame-like order around a 14x16 color image of Ciara. The pop star was scantily dressed in a sleek, gold thigh length skirt, a black sheer top and black net-style knee boots. "Hot!" was all Bop had said as he grinned, snapped his finger, and strutted back out the door.

And of course, in stark contrast to everyone else's contribution, anyone could guess that Jake had given a place of honor to two of his favorite Harlem Renaissance writers, Langston Hughes and Zora Neal Hurston. The two black and white, 8x10 calendar pages had been ripped out and placed in a cheap tin frame and carefully hung in a corner to the left of the room. Over the doorway, near the ceiling, JoJo had posted a generic, black and purple picture of a pair of black praying hands on velveteen, that he had paid three dollars for from a street vendor.

"To keep watch," he had quietly explained to Elbow and Bull who were present the day he brought it in. Only Cal Q and Bull had not gotten around to posting their celebrity.

For sure, they were a motley group, as different in personality as in ethnicity. As each had come to The Home, he had assumed a nickname, bestowed on him by the others. The name was descriptive, either of behavior, looks, or fighting style. Elbow and Bull were the only ones who already had their nicknames. Jake and JoJo were called by their given names.

Ricardo J. Estevan, alias, Elbow, the oldest of them all, just turned twenty-one, was nicknamed for his unorthodox fighting techniques. He was fast and hard, and took an uncanny delight in a good fight. "As long as it's necessary," Elbow claimed. "I don't look for trouble, but I won't turn my back when somebody is try'na take out my boys either."

Elbow was known to fight with a wide, circus-delight grin on his face. He often jabbed his boney elbow into his opponent's side. Though he owned both a gun and a knife, he had never used either. He had, however, spent six months in jail for selling weed and possessing a gun without a permit. He had also received a superficial knife wound when a member of a gang jumped him late one night as he left his job at the movie theater.

Elbow had been mistakenly identified as a member of the Whips. It was his fast, hard moves that saved his life that night. As unsettling and as frightening as that night was, if anyone were to ask Elbow which was worse, the stabbing or the time spent in jail, each time he would say the jail time.

"Jail didn't set right with me, bruhs. I mean, nobody in his right mind likes gettin' hurt, but that would heal." Elbow subconsciously rubbed the stab wound in his right side.

Though the scrimmages that the brothers had gotten into so far were, in his words, "necessary and clean," Elbow worried about the way some of them went out looking for trouble. He was especially concerned about Flippo's temper.

At about five foot, nine inches, Elbow was a bone-thin, mocha colored Puerto Rican who spoke English with very little accent. He was ten when his family moved to this country and settled in Oakland. At the time there were only six of them. In all there turned out to be nine. Elbow had no woe-is-me story about his earlier family life. In fact, he talked very little about himself.

"When you grow up in a family of nine children," he told them one day," you don't hang around long when your time comes. My old man always said, 'a man can take care of himself the minute he knows he's a man.' Been on my own since I turned sixteen. And that's that." Elbow made it clear that he didn't like to focus on his own story. It was the stories of his homies that concerned him.

As the brothers all agreed, Elbow was truly "down for The Home." What little he earned from his sometimes-on-sometimes-off job, cleaning the Grand Lake Movie Theater, he shared with anyone who came up short. It wasn't much, but it kept his little refrigerator full of lunch meats, cold drinks, and other basics. His tiny little grease-burned stove was there for any of them to "whip up a little Su'm Su'm to eat." Elbow was as soft for the brothers as he was hard on those who "messed over" them. He was a born protector.

It was no different the night fourteen year old JoJo came. "Hey lil' bruh, it ain't 'bout nothin'. Ain't 'bout no money, no games, no gimmicks. My place is yo' place lil' man'." Elbow had spoken as kindly, as assuredly as his tough exterior would allow that night he found JoJo curled up beneath the stair case, wrapped from head to toe in a rat-chewed, moldy canvas covering. The sleepy boy explained that he was waiting for somebody to come home. He wanted to meet Bull, the leader of the Whips. That cold California Bay Area night the brothers had adopted JoJo as the youngest member of the family.

Tailgate and Flippo had been the first to be brought into The Home. Bull recalled the night. He couldn't help but get a quiet chuckle out of the way Flippo and Tailgate all but bowed and went looking for a red carpet to lay out before him when they realized who he was.

Bull was leaving a party that night, over on Castro, in West Oakland. Since he was driving his brother's royal blue '99 Toyota Tercel and had drunk a few beers, he was being very careful to avoid the cops. When he saw these two spread-eagle against a patrol car, being aggressively searched, he instinctively became alert. Because of a poor relationship with the cops, he could not stop and covertly check out the situation as he sometimes did when he suspected that a brother was alone and in trouble.

Bull recalled circling the block twice before the cops released the two young men and drove off. "Records must have come up clean," he thought. "Or these two cops aren't hungry for any arrest tonight." Being doubly sure that the police car was clearly out of sight, Bull had driven up and offered Flippo and Tailgate a ride.

"Hey, man, I know you. You Bull Bullins. Right man? You hard, dawg." With a wide grin on his face, Flippo shot Bull a powerful dap. In a flash, Bull met the fist in the air. "Yeah, you one mean dude," Flippo laughed as he knocked his fist hard against Bull's. He began spilling out all the data about Bull that he had collected just by word of mouth. What Flippo left out, Tailgate filled in. The two boys couldn't end the litany of praises they had for Bull that night.

"It never changes," Bull mumbled, his mind returning to the quiet of the room." They always want me mean and hard. Three more shootings, one in East Oakland, and another in Richmond, all in two weeks - one 19 year old black male dead, one 17 year old Latino dead, and one eight year old female, caught in the crossfire, critically wounded. And the homeboys want action." Bull shook his head at the thought.

"Don't these dudes even know about the brothers dropped by the cops all across this country. This one shot and killed. Another one..." Bull stopped in mid-thought and drew a hard, deep breath." In two weeks alone, one brother in Tulsa. Another brother in North Carolina...And they wanna be a gang. Taking an even deeper breath, Bull shook as if to throw off the urge to cry. His face twisted into a painful grimace at his thoughts.

"We can't even go to church anymore, and not get shot down. Can't go pray. 'Action,' they want."

"Whee-ing-whee-ing-whee-whee-whee-whee-whee-ing!

The sound of a near-by police siren shook Bull free of his thoughts, and he jolted himself upright, sending the empty coke can careening across the room. Before he could walk to the window to check things out, he heard running footsteps. Bull recognized them as the sound of trouble.

Chapter Three

WILL THE REAL LEADER PLEASE STAND UP

If you don't help us, who will?"

No sooner had he thought the word, "trouble," that the brothers arrived. Knocking, thumping, panting, and sweating, they all tumbled in through the door. They were screaming and cursing. The frantic, angry shouts as they charged through the door, caused Bull to jolt to attention. He stood on guard for whatever trouble might accompany the brothers. His mind searched the near-by spot that kept Elbow's handgun concealed in the house. Only he and Elbow knew about the gun.

"Burners, man! They had burners! Flippo demonstrated how he got his name. He ran up to Bull, grabbed him in the collar and screamed like a madman in Bull's face. And they woulda smoked us if one of 'em hadn't recognized Elbow as part of your posse, man." Once more Flippo was flipping out.

"Flip!" Elbow's voice was low and serious. "Flip, ya losin' it, man. Remember what we talked about last night, dude. Cool is the word. We ain't no gang. Naw, they didn't touch us. They had fun chasin' us off their spot. That's 'cause they respect our leader, and they know that we ain't down for no gangbangin'. Bull didn't get out of the Whips with his life just to take us back there. We a family, man. Stop lookin' for fights before you get somebody killed." Elbow squeezed each of his hands into a tight fist and shook them desperately. "A family, man, a family."

Tailgate, Flippo's best friend in the group, was moved with compassion for him. He started over to Flippo while speaking directly to Bull. "Bull, man, Flip's right. We need some trainin'. It's been a long time since any of us had any real trainin'. We went out there for — some honeys — some fun, like everybody else. We didn't go lookin' for trouble. Trouble just found us, that's all. We just want some action - some excitement, man. Like everybody else. They our streets too. Ya' heard?"

Tailgate stretched out his hands in appeal, and then positioned himself directly in front of Bull again. Not yet satisfied, he went on talking. "We left our own cribs, cause our folk either not down with us, or they don't even know who we are — too busy doin' they own thing. Like in the case of lil' JoJo here — they can't be there. Some just plain too disappointed, like with my man Jake here. . ." He stared at Jake for a second, and left his statement hanging in the air.

Almost breathless, he continued. "We got to learn how to take care of ourselves and if fightin' is out there in that world, and we got to survive on these streets, then fightin' is what we got to do."

Tailgate paused to catch his breath. Hands slapping the air in frustration, he talked even faster. "Bull, man, if we don't learn how — if you our LEADER . . ." This last word he pronounced more like a question than a statement. "If you don't help us, who will?" Finally spent, Tailgate ended his speech abruptly, took a deep breath, let it out, dropped his arm and lowered his voice. "I'm tired of runnin' dude. That's all. A'ight? I'm tired of runnin' from it."

"I feel ya, Tailgate, man. I feel ya. But there's some other things to get worked up about right now. You and Flippo not the only ones with worries here," Bull answered.

"Other things? What kinda other things?" Flippo threw his hands in the air, and then folded them and took a defiant stance in front of Bull. "Just what kinda other things you

26

talkin' 'bout man?"

Bull glued his eyes on the lopsided, rusty, half-strung Venetian blinds attached to the only window in the room. For a moment he seemed to have left them stuck someplace in the back of his mind, as he once again entered his own world of memories. But as instantly as he left, he returned. His eyes fell instantly on JoJo.

"Take for instance, JoJo there. Come here JoJo," he beckoned, ignoring how close Flippo was in his face. JoJo immediately obeyed, standing at attention at Bull's side.

"How's school going, JoJo?"

JoJo squinted and dropped his head, saying nothing.

"What's JoJo and school got to do with this?" Flippo demanded.

"Everything," Bull answered. "JoJo's teacher is on his case and his daddy is threatening to send him down to Alabama to live with a great aunt who really doesn't want him there. We got to get JoJo back into school . . ."

"You a fine one to talk about going back to school, Bull," Flippo interrupted. In fact, can't none a us talk much about that 'cept maybe Jake. Can we Bull?"

"JoJo is the youngest here and if we're talking about being there for one another, we got to help him not make the same mistakes most of us made," Bull continued.

"Yeah, right," Flippo spat out the words as he flung his arm in the air, waving Bull off.

Staring first at Flippo and then at Tailgate, Bull spoke in a calm slower manner. "We'll chop this out later. Right now we got other business."

"Later. That's it. That's always it with you, Bull. I'm sick of you man. You playin' us Bull. You just playin' us man. I'm sick a you." Signaling to Tailgate, he headed toward the door. "Come on, Gate, let's bounce." Tailgate hesitated while Flippo stood there, glaring at Bull. The two boys were tight, Flippo and Tailgate. One was seldom seen without the other, and Flippo was obviously the leader of the two.

Flippo, known by his family as Dante Lewis, was a seventeen year old black kid from a foster family of five children, 3 boys and 2 girls. Of average height and size, he was a caramel color, with large brown eyes, and a slight mustache, which made him look more mature than his age.

Flippo was now living with his fourth family since age three. He was the third from the top. Elbow explained Flippo's constant rage with the boy's own words. "I've had four families too many. But that's a'ight; they don't want me. Well, I don't want them." He always ended this way. "And that's life — tough." It didn't seem to matter that Flippo's family was interested in him. Now and then one of his foster brothers would come looking for him, but Flippo would always ignore them or chase them away.

Tailgate, whose real name was Jorge Lopez, was also seventeen and had two younger sisters. Tailgate just could not accept spending all day in school. "The only thing school is good for, man, is the honeys. Anything else, I ain't got time," he explained when he first came to Elbow's. Almost six feet tall, with a thick frame and a winning smile, when he showed it, Tailgate had moved from Mexico with his family seven years ago. The Home was a place to get away from a father and mother who were relentless about making him go to school and get a part time job. "Be Somebody."

Besides their ages and need for The Home, Flippo and Tailgate had something else in common - their open rebellion against Bull. Both boys wanted to see The Home become something more than just a home. They wanted "action," but neither ever explained what "action" meant to them. For the most part, the others just understood it to mean excitement, and something important in their lives.

Known for his rear attacks in fights, Tailgate had relunc-tantly accepted his new name. He was not exactly proud of his cowardly methods of defending himself, but it was his Home name, and it made him feel that he belonged.

Taking in their frustration, Elbow made an attempt to come to the rescue of the angry twosome. "Maybe the men could use a little fun, Bull," Elbow considered. "Like a good party," he almost whispered, as he looked up knowingly at Bull. "Maybe a little family fun wouldn't hurt right about now." Elbow pause, waiting for a response from Bull.

"Everybody's edgy, dude. All these killings. And then their own personal stuff. It's a lot, man."

Bull stood, calm, wearing the usual control on his face and in his voice. He raised his right hand, fist clenched, into the air. "HOME! FACE!" He commanded with authority. Elbow grimaced subtly, but did not speak. He stood still and at attention. Like it or not, the command must be met. If he, next in command to Bull, did not obey, how could anyone expect the other brothers to, especially young JoJo. They had all agreed to this order of discipline. And since none of them wanted to be "tossed out" of The Home, for the most part, they all obeyed the house rules.

JoJo Calhoun, an almond colored fourteen year old, African American, with deep brown eyes and long soft corn rowed braids, moved into place within the circle links. JoJo's braids were pulled back from his face with a rubber band. His eyes often squinted as though he either needed glasses or had a bad headache. Now, steady squinting, he waited for further orders from Bull.

Taking orders was something JoJo wasn't afraid of. Unlike the others, he thrived on the guidance and protection of Bull and Elbow. Something in JoJo reached out for moth-ering — for being close to someone. He vaguely remembered his mother. The most he could tell the others was that when he was little, his mother had been attacked by some man late one night on the way home from work. She had gone to the parking garage near her job to get into her car when the brutal attack occurred.

Just after that she had died. Some say she took her own life. Others say she died of grief after what had happened to her. No one seemed to know for sure. It was something that JoJo's father did not talk about. It was his way of shielding the children from the horror. JoJo was about two years old when this awful thing happened. But his father had always been there, doing his best, working two jobs to raise JoJo and his two older sisters. He always assured them of how much their mother had loved them all.

JoJo never really felt close to his sisters. They were four and six years older than he, and always so busy. Both had been smart in school and had taken part in extracurricular activities. With his father at work all the time and his sisters on the go, JoJo spent a lot of time alone and more time scared.

Bull looked from one to the other of them as they formed a circle around him. He had previously explained to the guys that forming a line meant nothing but plain order, but a circle meant they'd hooked together — one for all. "There's more strength in the middle of a circle than at any one spot in a single line," he had taught them. This thought always made JoJo feel secure.

Jake, moving in his usual snail-like pace, pushed his one hundred, eighty pounds, six foot frame into the circle. He stood, a respectful grin tugging at the corner of his mouth. His oak colored curtained face suggested a vacancy. Behind his eyes was the usual far-away look characteristic of his countenance. Jake's mother had died of cancer when he was three. His father, a traveling computer salesman raised him, with the help of Jake's grandmother. Jake, being an only child who missed his father a lot, was just plain empty. He didn't fit in with other children; never did. The Home was truly his family.

Books were Jake's survival tools. He especially loved the poetry of Langston Hughes, Nikki Giovanni, Sonia Sanchez, Paul Laurence Dunbar, and Amiri Baraka. He took a special pride in his black heritage, and read documentaries every chance he got. The others claimed that Jake always looked spaced out because he kept his face in too many books.

When entering The Home for the first time, Jake was the only one who introduced himself with his full name, saying that a black man's name was his real claim, and that he'd better hold on to his own, because you never knew when he would need it.

"I'm Jake Lerone Blankenship," he'd proudly announced. Jake is for my granddaddy and my daddy, two true, proud black brothers. And with that, he'd abruptly taken his seat on the sunken sofa and held up a copy of Lerone Bennett, Jr.'s *Before The Mayflower*. He explained that Lerone Bennett Jr. was his daddy's favorite writer and the person for whom he, himself, had been named. Jake had inadvertently set his reputation as the intellectual of the group.

MopMan, the same age as Bull, was born into the world as Larry Knobles. Mop had a brother five years older than he, and long since out on his own. MopMan was nicknamed for his head of straggly, blonde hair that dangled around his keen, oval head, like a worn, unraveled rope mop. His otherwise smooth tan skin, usually had a small pimple, either on his nose or his forehead. He had a nervous habit of slinging his hair into place by a quick jerk of his head.

Mop was tough and keenly street-wise. He was close to Elbow, and, for the most part, he respected Bull. He often tried to coax the others into doing the same. He didn't say a lot, but he always did what he felt was expected of him. Being the only white member of the group did not bother Mop. Having grown up in East L.A. where his friends were mostly black or Latino, Mop was at home. Mop and his father "just couldn't make it," he had explained. His mother was "cool," but his dad had a temper and "wanted everything his way." Mop had been beaten many times by his father, and he just couldn't handle it anymore.

Being the only child left at home, he'd hated leaving his mother. But he seemed to have no other choice. He had started seeing himself fighting his dad back and he knew that this would hurt his mother. Besides, he had no desire to hit his own father. Rather than let it come to this, Mop had decided, like his brother before him, that it was time for him to go.

Bop, a.k.a. Jamal Jackson, was sixteen, but believed he was twenty or older. He was known for his want-to-be-cool, jive ways. Obeying Bulls order, he dragged-legged his dark brown angular body into the circle. Bop believed that his black pride was expressed in his lanky stride and his cool talk. His obedience to Bull was a bit some-timey, depending on his mood. Tonight, he was in Bull's corner, as he stood facing his leader, waiting for further orders. Besides Elbow, Bop was the only one of the group who had even gotten into trouble with the law. At fourteen, he was sent to Juvenile Hall for being "incorrigible." A series of run-a-ways, constant fighting, and smoking weed had gotten him sent away from his mother — his only family.

Cal Q, short for Cal-Quiet, was named for his quiet nature. Cal, whose name was really Calvin Willis, had a deep russet complexion. His skin had that rough, reddish tone, like he'd spent a lot of time outdoors. His lean body was a taunt knot. Short and slight of stature, Cal made up in strength and likeability what he lacked in size.

Cal was a black nineteen-year-old who had his own set of special needs. An only child, he had left his mother and father in Chicago to live with his grandmother in Oakland, but his grandmother took sick and had been moved to a nursing home. His original plan was to help his grand-mother, who was getting frail, and to attend a community college to study electronics. When his grandmother was moved out of her apartment, this left Cal out in the cold. He absolutely refused to return home, in spite of his mother's pleading.

Holding a job cleaning up an auto repair shop, he was able to keep a room for himself in a cheap, rundown residen-tial hotel; but most of his time was spent at The Home with the other guys. Cal thrived on the time he spent with the brothers, but he did not like Flippo's and Tailgate's desper-ate taste for fighting, or action, as they called it. He also did not like their arrogance and disrespect for Bull. In his own quiet way, Cal admired Bull, and thought he was a good leader simply because he was a "nice kinda brother."

Cal did not want trouble; he just wanted some place to be, away from an alcoholic father and a mother who escaped it all by working long hours every chance she got. Cal just hungered for company. He just wanted to "chill" with the homies. It was Cal who pushed for prohibition of drugs and hard liquor for the group. Cal was a whiz at fixing electronic equipment, but he just didn't like books a lot, and school just wasn't working out for him.

Everyone had come to attention except Flippo. Still ignoring the command, he began pacing the floor, muttering and tripping on the torn linoleum, while the others looked on. Tailgate made a clumsy effort with his head, to signal Flippo to come into the circle.

Chapter Four

The Home

It's a dog-eat-dog world out there

"HOME! FACE!" was the order no one dared to ignore. It was a typical Bull Bullins command. Translated, it meant, "men of this home come face together." This direct face-to-face communication reflected Bull Bullins himself. Bull was known for his straight-forwardness. It was part of the reason for his nickname. He didn't mince words or beat around the bush. He took the bull by the horns. He always tried to be fair when he could, even in fights he once got into. He aimed straight and hit hard.

When Bull struck, someone was bound to fall. Bull was the only member of the group who had been in an actual gang. It was he who started the group, and he who initiated the Cause. This was Bull's response to his sick mother's desperate plea about him and the gangs.

"Home! Face!" Bull stood in the middle of the circle of young men, giving Flippo a chance to come to his senses. "Home-face!" Bull's face was straight. His voice was low and controlled.

"It's family time, Flip — come on, now," Elbow appealed to Flip.

"No way!" Flippo ran to the door. "No way, man!" Pacing and panting, he pointed his finger at Bull. "Man you ain't right!" His breathing was heavy. His face drawn tight with rage. He paced frantically around the outside of the circle. "This ain't no family — we just a bunch of misfits with no leader — hanging between a gang and nowhere."

35

He took a fast breath and kept talking, "The in between gang. Yeah, that's what we are - stuck between a lot of nothing on one side and more nothing on the other side. Yeah!" Flippo sneered at Bull, and then made a desperate appeal to his buddy.

"Tell'em Tailgate. Since this is family — tell big daddy here what happened." He pointed at Bull. Tell 'em how you almost got it tonight, bruh." He appealed to his sidekick.

Before Tailgate could answer, Flippo turned, still huffing. "Bow, man, you did the best you could but even you need some trainin'. Cal. . ." Cutting off his own words, he continued his outburst. He paused, pacing, pleading, waiting, expecting some help from the others. No one came to his rescue. Tailgate gave Flippo a I-know-you-right, man look, but said nothing.

"Tell-em, Gate, man," Flippo shouted.

"Yeah, that's right, man — yeah. Tailgate shook his head and remained in his place in the circle.

"Y'all crazy!" Flippo's voice grew louder, with a few of his favorite obscenities flying from his mouth. "This cat ain't no leader! How can a brutha lead when he ain't never in The Home no more, huh? How can he lead when he ain't half here — always off somewhere else. And plus, what good is a leader who won't fight?"

Flippo was caught up in his own frenzy now. "Okay, so at first this was just suppose to be a home kinda place, somewhere to chill out when things got rough with the folks at the crib. It started out being somewhere to kick it when the whole world got down on you. But it's a war going on out there in those streets and somebody's always lookin' for a fight. Always tryin' to slice off a piece of somebody else."

Flippo paced and panted, looking first from one of the brothers to another. "Naw, I ain't down with that."

"Flip is right, Bull. We didn't ask for this messed up world, but we got to be ready for it, Bull, Man." Tailgate chimed in.

36

At this remark, JoJo turned his silent, still gaze on Tailgate. He took in a deep, solid breath and held it in his lungs. He set his eyes steadily on Tailgate. He shifted them, placing his stare on Flippo, then on Bull, and back to Flippo. After he'd completed the circle with his eyes, JoJo released a loud, huffy breath, all the while remaining at stilted attention.

Y'all shut up," Bop demanded as he slid up closer to Bull. "Let's hear what Bull got to tell us anyway."

"Forget it, Bull," Flippo screamed at him. "You promised us some trainin', Bull, man. You said we'd learn to take care of ourselves so we won't have to be scared of nobody. You promised."

"Okay, okay," Bull sauntered over to Flippo. He grabbed him by his collar and shoved him into the center of the gang. "Now, you want to be a hard punk — you speak. You got so much to say. Talk. And it better be good. Sit down, men." He turned and beckoned to the others. "Flippo here has something more important to say. Holla' at us, Flip."

Everyone sat, some more hesitantly than others. They were all relieved that Bull did not take Flippo by the horns this time. The group really did not like fighting among themselves. They knew that it defeated the Cause. The real Cause, as for Bull and most of the brothers was surviving the streets and providing a safe harbor for one another. They knew each other's stories and promised to be there for each other. The real Cause was brotherhood. Everyone knew that fighting one another defeated the Cause.

They sat while Flippo wind-gusted Bull. His voice was a thunderstorm, slapping hot air at Bull's ego. Flippo worked hard at stripping Bull of all of his rights to be their leader. His eyes sent lightning flashes to melt away Bull's pride. He spat out bitter contempt. Hot gusty words flew from Flippo's mouth. But Bull stood stern and steady. Once more he allowed Flippo his tornado. This was not the first such tantrum, nor was it likely to be the last that Flippo had thrown with Bull.

The winds of his anger having died down a bit, Flippo sank against the wall and stared hotly at Bull.

"Fighting," Bull faced Flippo sternly. "Is that all we joined together to do? Is that what you want your whole life to be about? Flip? Or. . ."

"Or what?" Tailgate took up the issue. "Or die? We didn't make that dog-eat-dog world out there any more than you did, or Elbow or Cal or JoJo did. But we all got to live in it, man. Somebody messed it up for me, for you, for all us." Caught up in the impact of his own emotions, Tailgate sprang to his feet and pointed his finger out toward the street. He tried hard to control the tremble in his raised voice.

Tailgate went on, becoming emotionally charged again as he talked. "Dog-eat-dog. That's what it is. The hardest, the quickest, and the meanest man gets the biggest bites. You either fight or gon' be a feast for the other side. You fight or you die. You learn to smoke 'em or you wait for them to smoke you. It's that simple, man. You know it. You been there Bull. You know better than anybody."

It had come to this, clear and simple. From where Tailgate and Flippo stood, it's that simple. Fighting was equal to eating. A dog-eat-dog world they called it; a philosophy as old as fighting itself. It meant being out there, open, to all kinds of pain. "Dog-eat-dog," a philosophy that allowed you to win, or caused you to lose. It was the only belief system they knew. Yes, Bull knew that Tailgate was right; he had been there. It was exactly what he'd finally escaped, what he'd hoped to save them from. His whole purpose for them now was to save them from the bloodshed that gang life brought. It's what his Mama begged him to leave behind.

Bull could not deny it. They looked to him for answers. He was Bull Bullins. Many had feared him. His fellow members basically idolized him. Girls loved him. He commanded both fear and love at the same time; something few people on this earth could do. There they were, huddled together, aching and trying not to show it. His power did not give him control over their pain; it only allowed him to look at it, and now and then reach out to touch it.

On one hand he was angry at Flippo. On the other hand he was disturbed at himself for letting them see his own doubt. Had they heard the echoes of his earlier thoughts? Had they heard his questions resound, clanging loud above the din of their fight? Had they seen the pieces of glass in his mind, or noticed the scratches they made on his face?

A decision had to be made. Either he would help them or he would not. Either he'd stand by them as their leader and try to teach them, or he'd follow his heart to places, people, and things which even he didn't understand yet. Sure, he realized that what they wanted from him at the start was more than just a "place." He'd been the tough-and-ready-to-kick-butt, bad boy, Bull Bullins at that point. They needed that part of him.

But now — now, things were changing, and much too fast for him to sort out in front of them. When did it all begin to change? The first six months or so were spent just hanging together, getting away from the world, and escaping troubled homes. They use to laugh more, play dominoes, order Round Table pizza with Elbow's coupons. They use to chop it up about past fights. He knew that they were enjoying his reputation, and felt secure with it, but no one had pushed to become a street gang then.

Flippo. It all came from Flippo. And of course, what Flippo wanted, Tailgate wanted, whether he really wanted it or not.

Bull realized that he was standing silent before them. He yielded to the torment that tore at his mind and at his heart. It ripped at his gut. He was unable to give them the answers they needed so badly. For the very first time, he simply did not have the answer. He sent each of them a calm deliberate stare. He moved toward the door. Standing in the dead silence, with his hand gripping the doorknob, Bull inhaled deeply, held it for a bit, and blew it out in a spurt. Without saying a word, he turned and walked slowly out the door.

Chapter Five

AND WHAT ABOUT MAMA?

Her mind is a prison, and she's locked her pain up in it.

Out on the street Bull could think, so he thought. Somehow the honking horns, the periodic wail of a siren, and the busy chatter of passersby distracted him . The pungent, moist scent from a near-by fast food place wafted through the air, reminding him of how long it had been since he ate. The night sounds, smells and sights muffled the clanging noise of his own thoughts, and lessened the throbbing pain. The angry din of his homeboys left behind, he just needed to clear his mind.

For a while he concentrated only on the loud clicking of his boot heels on the pavement. Bull still insisted on wearing metal taps on the heels and soles of his shoes. It was a practice their daddy started when they were all just little boys. He and his brothers Jay and Hal would make rhythmic sounds on the concrete, pounding their feet hard on every sidewalk grate they passed. Their parents would laugh at the boy's dance antics, calling them the future Jackson Five.

His parents use to laugh a lot. They were close and spent a lot of time together, as well as quality time with the boys. They were a happy family. People wondered how he and Jay ever got caught up in the streets. Their parents gave them a good childhood. There were always trips to Knowland Zoo, Dimond Park, Chinatown in San Francisco, and Tilden Park in Berkeley. In fact there wasn't a park in all of the Bay Area that the Bullins family hadn't spread a blanket, a basket of fried chicken and ice cold Capri Sun. There had even been a couple of trips to Disneyland, in Southern California. The Bullins boys didn't suffer from attention from their parents.

"The good ole' days," Bull mumbled sadly.

In answer to why their eldest and youngest sons were attracted to gang life, Mr. Bullins had simply thrown up his hands and concluded, "pressure, just plain peer pressure." Mrs. Bullins, on the other hand, had declared "something is eating at our boys. We got to find out, honey. We just got to find out."

"Jay follows the fun and excitement," Mr. Bullins had admitted. "Always, did. Even down in the low grades. It didn't matter how much trouble they ended up in. Once Jay calls you his friend, you can do no wrong. He seems to always have something to prove to his friends."

"Jay's a good boy. Warm, caring. Would give you the shirt off his back." Mrs. Bullins had quickly come to her eldest son's defense. " But how could a child so tender with animals be so attracted to such a hard and mean life," She questioned. "Like that dead bird he found under a tree in Tilden Park that day. What was he, five, six?" Not waiting for an answer from her husband, Mrs. Bullins continued. "That boy must have cried and stroked that bird a full hour."

"Jay follows the fast moving crowd and Sherman follows the brother he looks up to more than anyone in this world. That's why we just got to get them out of Oakland. Got to send both of them away." Mr. Bullins hung his head and grew quiet.

Bull's steps were swift and sure as he quickly pulled himself out of his reverie. He didn't know where he was headed. He just needed to be alone. He needed to be outside.

As he walked, his thoughts began to pan out. He could make a little sense alone, lost in the crowd. As a light spring night mist began to dampen the concrete, the cool East Bay air opened his mind. The truth of the matter was that the brothers needed the old Bull back. They needed the horn-gripper, the woman's man, the smooth player who had more than his share of honeys, and just as many fights. They needed his old gang image badly. It made them feel safe, and he couldn't blame them.

Were they really expected to understand the lie in him? How could he tell them that he'd accepted their role for him because at the time he was too scared and insecure himself to say no. It's hard to say no to a kingship when you're feeling lost yourself. Furthermore, how could he explain to them that he bled inside too. In fact, he bled twice as much, some for himself, and some for them. No way would Bull tell the brothers that somebody in him had to get out, or that somebody might bleed to death.

"We wear the mask." He could hear Jake's voice quoting the poet, Paul Laurence Dunbar. The words got caught up in the clicking of his shoes on concrete. They echoed through the sidewalk grate and did a triple bounce off every building facade he passed.

"Will the real Mr. Bullins please hold my hand." He heard Cheri's voice in his head. "Come on, Sherman." She did not like calling him Bull. "Come on. Don't be afraid of the soft beating of your heart. You're so used to the knocking and pounding that goes on inside of you. Give the quiet beats a chance." Cheri had whispered. She was new in his life, and already she was stuck in his head. Yet, even with her he guarded his heart.

"We wear the mask." Cheri would say that about him, that's for sure.

"Come back, man. You don't have to be Bull all your life." Hal's words echoed in his head. Everyone had advice for him, but no one could give him the answers.

The lights were on when Bull reached the apartment he shared with Hal, about an hour later. He didn't feel up to his brother's lecturing tonight. Running into Mack didn't help his mood at all. He hesitated at the steps, thinking to turn back. Where would he go? Elbow wouldn't be happy to see him right now, the way he'd walked off in the middle of a meeting. For the moment, he was a deserter to the brothers. Thinking that maybe Hal had been too tired and gone to bed, Bull fished for his key. He unlocked the door and went inside.

"Message," Hal shouted at him from the bathroom, muttering through a mouth full of Crest. "On the 'frig. Said she'd call you tomorrow. Guess you're not giving out your cell number, huh." Hal paused, waiting for a response from Bull. Asked for "Sherman." Hal exaggerated Bull's real name. This time his mouth was clear of the tooth paste.

"Thanks," Bull shouted back to him. Before he could make up his bed on the sofa, Hal was at his heels.

"You know I don't pry into your private life, little brother. But she did sound nice. Am I being too nosey when I ask who she is?"

Bull fought back a grimace. "Oh, just someone I know from the studio. Just a friend."

"Mmmnn, oh well, it's your secret, just like ninety-nine percent of your life is a secret."

Hal started to his room and stopped suddenly, turning to Bull. "Incidentally . ." He hesitated, then went on speaking deliberately, almost accusingly. "Incidentally, do your brothers . . ." Hal twisted the word "brothers" around on his lips a bit, and dampened it with sarcasm, before he threw it at Bull. "Do your brothers know about your part-time job at Channel 2? And what about your night classes you plan to take, to get your GED? Or do you have secrets from them too?" Hal didn't pause for an answer.

"How long, Sherman? How long will you keep the brick walls up around yourself, shutting everybody out." Taking his brother's silence as a sign that he just might be penetrating that wall, Hal kept talking.

"I'm proud that you had the strength and fortitude to leave the Whips, Sher, but why this wall. Mama, me, even your own partners out there. What's eating at you, dude? You're out Sher. You're free! Why won't you let anyone near you?"

Still interpreting Bull's silence as a green light, Hal continued. "When did it change, Sherman? Even when you were still in with the Whips, and only came by the house now and then, you talked to me more than you do now." Hal paused for a moment, as though collecting his thoughts.

"Do you remember when you left the Whips, and several of the members threatened your life?"

Bull glared at his brother, but said nothing.

"There was no wall between us then, Sherman."

"You communicated with Boxer, not with me." Bull seemed to gag on his own words. He said nothing further.

"That might be, but Boxer came here to talk to you and me. He came to assure you that because you had saved his little brother from an attack by a rival gang member, he owed you. And that, being leader of the Whips, he could personally promise you that you could have out and no one would touch you."

Bull looked at his brother. This time he held his stare in heated animation. The veins in his neck contracted, accurately addressing his rising anger. But Bull held his tongue. He did not like being reminded about those times. He hated it when anyone, Hal, in particular, brought up the Whips.

"You were for-real then, man." Hal ignored the change in his brother's countenance. "I'm scared, Hal, man. I'm scared." These were your words Sherman. They were real words. You were more for-real then, Sher.

Hal waited. He knew that his brother would have to respond to what he had just said. But still, Bull did not speak. He just stood, staring at his brother.

You were the Sherman I used to know, then man." Hal paused, sighed and continued. "Where is my brother? Where is Sherman Bullins? I WANT HIM BACK!" He sud-

45

denly shouted.

Bull tried to ignore the pulsating at the back of his neck. He tried to ignore the heat in his face. With artificial control in his voice, he spoke. "Ease off, Hal. Just ease off tonight. I have things to think about. I'm tired, and I'd like to go to bed. Just chill, Hal. Okay?"

"Come off it, Sherman. Don't pull that "off my back" scene with me tonight. There's plenty on my mind too, and it all has to do with you. Hal hesitated, bit his lip and continued. "It's also about Mama, Sherman. Remember her?"

Before Hal could get the words out of his mouth, Bull spun around, charged across the room like a panther on a prey, and grabbed his brother by the collar. "Don't you ever run that game on me again. Every time you want to run my life you throw Mama up at me."

Hal gripped Bull's hands and pulled them loose of his collar, and then he pushed Bull back away from him. He stretched his lanky frame to its full, six feet, two inches. Hal stood two inches taller than Bull. Both boys had gotten their height and their mahogany skin color from their father, while Jay, also of slight built, had gotten his medium height and buff complexion from his mother.

A physical confrontation between the two would most likely have yielded an even match; but since their mother's illness, the brothers had avoided squabbles and fights between them. Allowing his brother time to compose himself, Hal stared in disbelief at Bull.

"Chill, Sherman. We got to have this out now."

"I told you, man. I told you well in advance that I can't handle you and your motherly advice and criticism tonight. I have other things to deal with right now. Can't you ever respect where I'm coming from? Can't you ever listen?" Bull launched for the door. Hal was fast behind and caught him by the shoulder falling down in a tangle. Before he could think about it, Bull swang around and pushed his brother back.

"Oh, okay, so it's like that - so you want to fight me now, huh? You didn't get enough when you were out there. Okay. Come on, lil' brother. Take your best swing. I guess I got enough of it in me to take you on." Hal pushed Bull's shoulder, "You want a piece of me that bad, Sher? Come on, man. Get it out once and for all." He pushed his brother again.

This was more than Bull could handle. The stress of his day caught up with him, and he took a hard swing at Hal. The punch landed on Hal's right shoulder. The brothers tussled across the floor. Suddenly, Bull jumped up and started screaming at his brother. "No. I won't go there. No!" He rushed to the sofa and sat, holding out his open palm at his brother. "You won't drive me back out there. No! I stopped fighting. I won't fight." Bull Bullins dropped his head into his hands.

Pulling himself from the floor, Hal sat next to his brother.

"Sherman, man, the last thing I want you to do is fight. We lost one brother to the streets already. But check this, Sherman. Check this. Mama needs to see you. She's been in that place for a year, and you haven't been to see her but twice." He paused and stared softly at his younger brother. He saw the tears glisten in Bull's eyes. He knew that the subject of their mother always caused Sherman to run, to get angry, all in an effort to blot it out. This time Hal was determined not to let Bull escape talking about their mother.

Bull stood and walked to the door. "I can't Hal. I just can't see. . ."

"Sit down, Sher. Come on, man, sit down. We don't have to fight." He patted the sofa. "Can't we finally talk about it, Sherman? I'm Hal, not your enemy. I'm not a member of the Whips and I'm not a cop. I'm Hal. Don't you think seeing Mama that way hurts me too? Huh?" Hal extended his arm toward the sofa again. "What about it, Sher?"

47

Bull stood at the half open door. His head rested lightly against the cool wood. He blinked, breathed deeply, and raised his hand to his eye. He hadn't even realized that he was crying. Slowly he wiped away the evidence, walked quietly to the sofa, and sat down.

The two brothers talked late into the night. They recalled the events that led up to the loss of their older brother, and how all of it sent their mother into a state of shock. They discussed how she'd just plain escaped the pain of it by letting go of her mind. Mrs. Bullins had to be committed to an asylum for the mentally disturbed shortly after the nightmare event that changed all of their lives.

They talked about the time Jay was arrested, how he was brought in one night after a shooting in West Oakland. Having a reliable witness that he was on the other side of town the night of the shooting, and having no gun on him, Jay was set free after being detained half the night. As it often turns out with gang related shootings in black and Latino neighborhoods, no further arrests were made in the case.

"That's when I really started thinking," Bull confessed to his brother. "Right then and there I started thinking how there would always be youth in the streets, and that somebody had to teach them a better way. That somebody had to be there for them. But..." Bull grew silent. "But I just wasn't ready. I just wasn't ready. I didn't want to leave Jay. I..."

"I know," Hal whispered. I know, man."

Jay was always Sherman's idol. As early as ten years old, Jay had shown signs of being attracted to the streets, and later Bull had followed his brother in that direction. But though his brother's death served to make him a great hero in the eyes of the other members of his gang, it brought Bull in off the streets. Bull did not want to see any more brothers shot down. Somebody had to be there and he knew the streets. It was on him. His mother's words had sealed the deal for him.

"Mama needs to see you, Sher."

"See me? She doesn't even know me anymore. I can't stand seeing that long distance stare in her eyes. Why go on trying to talk to a shell? Man, she's not Mama anymore." Bull buried his face in his hands and tensed his body.

"Man, she. . . she's . . . she's like a zombie," he continued. She doesn't even know that I'm there, Hal. Her mind is a prison and she's locked her pain up in it." He paused, took a deep breath, and turned his head away from his brother. Slowly, he breathed. When he turned back and spoke to Hal, his face had a steely, unnatural kind of calmness. His voice was low and controlled. "Mama is as good as dead."

Though shocked at his brother's words, Hal remained calm. His voice was low and even, laced with irritated sympathy.

"But she's not. She's alive, Sherman, and like it or not she's still your mother. You can't go running from that. You can't blot her out and hope she disappears, Sherman. Go see her, man. Go see Mama."

When they had exhausted themselves with talk, the two brothers went to bed. Listening to the quiet, even snores of Hal from the one bedroom, Bull lay tensed. He needed to blot out Hal's words. They awakened fresh pain in him. He had enough already.

"Teach them to survive within the law," Hal had often insisted. Tell them to go back to school."

How could he tell the brothers to do something he could hardly decide to do for himself, return to school and get their lives together — make something of themselves. He was barely moving himself in that direction.

And Mama. He knew that he could not go on treating her as though she didn't exist. Quickly Bull pushed aside the picture that was forming in his mind. It was the picture of him about five years old, laughing up in his mother's eyes

while she read him to sleep: "The Little Train that Could."
He didn't want to see the picture. The light in those eyes was
not there anymore, so he did not want to see them in his
mind. It hurt too deeply. Quickly he turned his mind from it
and focused it on some plans for the brothers. Finally, Bull
drifted off to sleep.

*Gradually, through a white-gray mist, another picture
formed. He saw a figure of a woman walking up a steep hill.
The hill was full of deep green grass. His eyes followed the
figure as she slowly, painstakingly placed one foot in front
of the other until she reached the top of the grassy knoll.
Turning counter clockwise the figure extended her hands
toward Bull and waved for him to climb the hill.*

*Out of nowhere, Bull thought he heard a train sound in
the distance. Looking around him, he only noticed a cloud of
fog settling over the hill, covering the woman standing there
beckoning to him.*

"I can't," Bull shouted up to her. "I can't do it."

*"There is no such thing as can't, Sherman. There is no
such thing as can't." Again the figure reached out her hand
to him.*

*"She called my name," Bull thought, "How does she
know me? Who is she?"*

*Lured by the comforting sound of the woman's voice,
Bull began to climb. Just as he reached the center, he
thought he saw a train in the distance, behind the figure.
Before Bull could turn and run back down or up toward the
figure on the top, the train began ascending the hill, heading
directly at the figure of the woman at the top. Bull felt chill,
and then drops of hot perspiration poured down his face.
Panicking, he tried to rush to save the woman, but his feet
would not move. His body had become a ton of bricks. All he
could do was watch and scream to her to get out of the way.*

*As the train gained momentum, a cloud of fog covered
the hill and the woman, but not before Bull realized who the*

woman was. More desperately, he tried to move to save her from the train. The cloud of mist became denser and settled lower. The train whistle grew louder and the rumbling of its wheels was unbearable to Bull's ears. Though it approached a grassy hill, the wheels sounded like steel on metal. Closer and closer it came. Again Bull tried to pull himself up the hill to her. "Mama, mama, mama. . ." He heard himself scream as the fog closed in. "Mama!"

"Sherman. Sherman! Wake up, Sherman. It's me Hal. Wake up!" Shaking his brother, Hal assured him. "You were dreaming man. You called out to Mama. It's alright."

Bull sat up. His t-shirt was soaked from sweat. His body felt numb. He thought he was going to be sick.

"It was awful, Hal. Man it was awful. That train. At first, I felt good when I saw her. I saw Mama, Hal." Bull almost choked on his words. "And then that train...that train." With that, Bull became quiet. The brothers sat in complete silence, with Hal's hand rested assuredly on his younger brother's shoulder. They sat this way until the shadow of Bull's nightmare loosened its grip, and the two returned to their beds.

Chapter Six

ON THE # 39 BUS

Responsibility is a killer sometimes, man

It must have been close to 8:00 AM the next morning when Bull awoke suddenly. He felt that he had tossed and turned all night. His mind was groggy and his body felt heavy. It was like he'd just pulled himself up from the water after a long swim. The image of his mother still in his mind, Bull let himself roll to the edge of the couch. Slowly dragging himself up, he sat with his head in his hands.

Eventually, he rose from the couch. Like a mother trying to avoid awakening her sleeping baby, he tip-toed into the bathroom. As he brushed his teeth and took a quick shower, snapshots from last night's dream flashed through his mind. Throwing on a pair of faded black Levi jeans and a plain white tee-shirt, he prepared to leave the house.

"Mama," he whispered, almost unconsciously. Shaking himself back to the present, he softly opened the front door. One thing Bull did not want was to wake up Hal. He couldn't stand anymore of his brother's questions and demands this morning.

"I need some air. Gotta get out," he muttered, as he reached for his dark blue hoodie. "Plenty of time before I meet Cheri."

The two had agreed on an early morning meeting in Dimond Park, the area where Cheri lived in a large white stucco with her parents. They would sit in the quiet morning, enjoying just being together alone before Cheri left for an all-day outing with her family. The Johnstons often had family outings. Today they would be taking a ferry across the Bay to Sausalito for lunch.

"Just like we used to do." Bull forced back the memories of him, his brothers, and his parents, in the park, eating barbecue doused with his daddy's special homemade sauce. He could see them playing volleyball, riding over to San Francisco to hang out in Chinatown, or just cruising and looking at the sights of the Bay Area.

Though he had only a couple of blocks to walk to catch the 39 to go up Fruitvale to the Dimond Area, Bull made a mad dash out of the house. He didn't have to wait long. In all of 10 minutes he was settled on his bus heading to the park.

As the 39 rumbled, spat exhaust, made stops and started again, Bull found his mind absorbed with thoughts of Cheri. In spite of his reluctance, Cheri Johnston had in two short months, come closer than any girl to stealing Bull's heart. She had gotten him to thinking more seriously about his life. It was Cheri, beautiful, cinnamon colored sister, with short curly black hair and brown eyes that sparkled when she laughed. In fact, it was Cheri's warm smile and easy laughter that had attracted Bull to her that Sunday evening he first met her in the park.

He was alone. She was alone. She had struck up a conversation with him. It was then she'd told him that she worked at television station, Channel 2. They'd talked for two hours that day. Bull had never talked to any girl that long, nor in the way he'd talked to Cheri.

Bull did not know what key Cheri had used to unlock that laughing, talking place in him, but she had done it. Before he realized it he had told Cheri Johnston some things about himself he had never dared think in the presence of other girls. She was so different from the others. Laughter from the others did not ring as softly and sweetly. While most girls talked about what they wanted him to buy them or do for them, Cheri talked about what Bull could do for himself.

Passing Peet's Coffee to the left, Bull knew that Ly-Luck Chinese Restaurant and the public library were just ahead and he should get ready to get off the bus. As the 39 approached MacArthur Boulevard, the last stop before the park, Bull stood and walked to the door. The bus screeched to an abrupt stop, almost knocking him off his feet. "Watch it man," Bull mumbled as he jumped the step to the street.

Feeling hungry, he decided to swing by Safeway to pick up a couple of doughnuts and some coffee for him and Cheri. Remembering that he was short on cash, he decided to make a stop at an ATM.

"Here a bank, there a bank," he sang as he noted a Chase, a Wells Fargo, and a Citi Bank all on the same corner where he exited the bus. A distinguished looking middle aged- black man was approaching the Wells Fargo ATM. A young white woman in her late 20's, with her sandy blonde hair in a pinned-up pony tail, jogged in place as she retrieved her cash from the Chase machine. Bull smiled and shook his head good-naturedly as he read the bold white letters on her purple sweat shirt: "Running is love on two feet."

Instantly Bull crossed to the park side of the street, trotting carefully around a red Chevy pickup with a broad, white, handmade sign that read JOSE'S LANDSCAPE scrolled across both sides. Bull quickly made his way to the Bank of America and positioned himself in front of the ATM machine. There was no one to detain him, so he was able to access his account quickly. Being preoccupied with his transaction, Bull did not see the young man come up behind him. All of a sudden he felt something hard and cold pressed into his back. He knew what it was. He was being robbed.

"Gi' me yo' wallet. C'mon, hurry up. I ain't playin' wit chu."

The voice sounded familiar. It had a gruff edge to it. There was only one person that he knew with a voice like that. "Gi' me yo' wallet," the gruff voice repeated. Slowly Bull pulled his wallet from his jeans pocket and reached it back to the gunman.

"Now walk away . . ." the voice began. Bull was certain now. He had no doubt who was holding a gun on him.

"Hawkeye — it's Bull."

Quickly, Hawkeye spun Bull around to face him.

"Bull — naw man! Naw!"

There stood Hawkeye, mouth open, wearing that same old raggedy black do-rag beneath a green and yellow Oakland A's baseball cap, turned to the right side of his head.

Hawkeye stuffed his gun into his pocket and backed away, thrusting Bull's wallet back into Bull's hand, and suddenly turned and ran.

Bull stared after him. He was both shocked and relieved. It wasn't the first time he had had a gun aimed at him. But now that he was off the streets, he had stopped thinking about ways it could happen.

"Hawkeye's still playing gangsta'. Does it ever really change?"

Pensively, Bull walked, now noticing nothing around him, slowly making his way to Dimond Park. He just wanted to sit and ease his rapidly beating heart. This was no way to start a day. No doubt, the sight of Cheri would calm him.

Before he realized it, Bull had reached Dimond Park. Still feeling annoyed over his ATM encounter with Hawkeye, he flopped down on the red brick construction at the entrance of the park. The splashes of purple, fuchsia, white and yellow flowers arranged around the entrance escaped his attention. Voices drifted on the light morning breeze as the park filled with people.

Dimond Park was a popular Saturday morning hangout. It was just the place he needed this morning. The hushed, laid-back tones of a gathering community promised to bring Bull around. He took a deep breath, pulling the fresh air into his lungs and letting it out in a quick huff. He felt better already. When Cheri showed up, things would be great.

A short time later, Bull and Cheri were walking hand in hand into the park, past the grove of trees to the left, adjacent to an open grassy play area. They paused for a moment to watch a group of middle school boys kick a soccer ball around.

"Wanna play," Cheri asked him, laughing. Without a word he gently pulled her to him and planted a light kiss on her lips.

"I'm scared of those lil' homies." Soccer ain't my game," he laughed.

Falling quiet again, the two continued their walk around the park. They meandered along the path that ran along the partially dried creek, up behind the tennis court, along the path of thick green shrubbery, and made their way back to the grove of shady trees near the entrance of the park.

The park was alive now with women pushing babies in strollers, small children batting balloons into the air, families setting up tables and heating up the barbeque grills scattered within the perimeter of tall, billowing trees. Sitting alone under an Elderberry tree was a senior age woman, reading a book and eating red grapes from a plastic grocery bag.

"Right here," Cheri said suddenly. "This is a good spot."

At her directions, Bull carefully spread Cheri's blanket that he had been carrying under his arms. The trouble at The Home, his fight with Hal, the dream of his mother, Hawkeye - it all faded into nothingness, there under the large Willow tree where he sat with his new, beautiful girl friend. The knots in his stomach were gone. Taking a deep breath and slowly letting it out, he lay back and stretched himself full length on the blanket, gently pulling Cheri with him. Saying nothing for minutes, the two lie gazing up at the still, azure sky. Not a cloud in sight. It was the perfect day to chill with his girl. It was, that is, until she asked him to come to her house to meet her parents.

"Cheri, no. Not after Hawkeye. Not after…He paused. "It's just not the right time," he protested.

"If not now, when," she gently insisted. My folks won't bite you."

"Oh yeah," he said. Jolting himself up to a sitting position, he looked back at her. "That's because they haven't met the boy from the ghetto yet," he half teased.

"Stop saying that," she winced, as she sat up and wrapped her arms around his waist. "There are ghettoes, as they called them, in every community; red, black, brown, yellow, white – you name it."

"You told me yourself that your dad knew my name and all about my brother, Jay. He even told you he didn't like the idea of you spending time with me. So why would you pull me into the lion's mouth," he questioned.

Cheri didn't say anything else. She simply stood up and waited for him to do the same. As though Bull were not present, Cheri started walking in the direction of the entrance. Bull stood, snatched up the blanket, and joined her. Grabbing his hand, Cheri led Bull across Fruitvale, over to Lyman Road, just in front of the park.

When they reached the large white stucco where the Johnstons lived, Mr. Johnston was in the front yard, stooped over, picking up the morning paper. Mrs. Johnston stood with the door screen half open, sipping coffee from a mug, shouting something to Mr. Johnston. The scene that followed was quick and ugly.

Mama, Daddy, this is Sherman Bullins. I told you…"

"And I told you that I didn't want you hanging around with street thugs," Mr. Johnston growled, ignoring the hand that Bull extended to him.

"Dave!" Mrs. Johnston gasped from the door.

"Daddy! Cheri cried.

"We have nothing to shake on, young man. We don't need your kind around here. Stay away from my daughter." The big, burly man turned and pounced back into the house, calling for Cheri to follow him.

Immediately, Bull turned, spouting a quick and angry goodbye to Cheri. Without even looking back, he went to his bus stop, at the corner of MacArthur and Fruitvale, to catch the number 39 back down Fruitvale toward home. He could not tell how long he had waited, but after several other buses had come and gone, he looked up and saw the 39 making its way toward him.

Once the bus had completed its jerky, screeching stop, Bull hopped on, paid his fare and chose a seat in the rear. In desperate need of some quiet space, he laid his head back on the leather cushion and closed his eyes. He yielded to the hustling and bustling sounds of passengers getting on and off the bus, connecting with the regular puffs from the air brakes.

"I think I can. I think I can. I think I can." One minute the singsong voice of his mother rang through his head, as he pictured himself, a boy of four or five, leaning on his mother's lap as she read "The Little Engine That Could" for the third consecutive time. The dream, the fog, his mother's voice – it all became jumbled again.

Somewhere in the mix, he heard the voice of Hawkeye at the ATM machine, 'Gi' me 'yo wallet." Between the two Bull could hear Hal insisting, "Go see Mama, man." Somewhere far in the distance in his mind he heard the voices of the homeboys, shouting, "We need some trainin', "man." His homeboys voices seemed to mingle with that of Mr. Johnston's, "We don't need your kind around here."

Around and around they went. All of the voices, all at one time. For a second Bull felt dizzy, like he did when his daddy would swing him around in the air making his stomach dance, causing him to laugh uncontrollably. Only this dizzy was sickening.

"Hey bruh," Cal Q sang as he plopped down on the seat next to Bull." Whassup?"

Caught completely off guard by Cal's abrupt appearance, Bull jolted to attention. "Q, ma' man!" he instantaneously tapped his fist against Cal's extended fist. "Whassup?"

"You got it," Cal chimed.

"So, what are you doing on The 39 on a Saturday morning?"

"I was gonna ask you the same thing," Cal said.

"Oh, just got up cause I couldn't sleep. Oh, yeah, and to give an old acquaintance a chance to poke a gun in my back at the ATM. You know, stuff like that. Usual Saturday morning adventure."

"You been drinkin' man?"

"Not even a cup of coffee," Bull said. "Really, Cal, I got held up right there at the ATM machine at Bank of America, across from the Safeway Center."

"You serious, huh, man. They get anything from you?"

Bull gave Cal a play-by-play account of the attempted robbery.

"Didn't get a thin dime," Bull proudly concluded.

"And you knew the dude?"

"He's not one that I'm proud of knowing, but yeah. Hawkeye's a wanna-be bad boy. I knew him on the streets. Never did get hooked up with a gang. Just went around snatching women's purses and beating up on kids. I guess today was suppose to be his graduation into the big time."

Both boys were quiet for a long time.

60

Bull broke the silence. "Hawkeye is just the kind of brother I don't wannna see my boys at The Home become."

"Flippo — huh?"

"Yeah," was all Bull answered.

Again, silence fell between them.

"Where're you heading," Bull asked?

Cal-Q shifted in his seat and looked out the window.

"Hey Q, man, you give a brother the impression that you don't wannna talk no more?"

"Ah, I'm just trippin', man. Saturday, and all, you know." Cal shrugged and looked out the window again.

"Yeah, alright," Bull answered with a shrug

Bull rested his head on the back of his seat and closed his eyes, while Cal just stared out of the window. A frown slowly crossed his face, and he looked as though he were fighting to hold back a dam of tears.

"If I tell you something, Bull, will you keep it a secret? I mean, like between you and me. Nobody else. Just me and you." Cal stared out of the window as he spoke.

Bull quickly opened his eyes and sat up. He looked directly at Cal, who was now looking directly at him.

"Cal, you look like you just lost your best friend, man. You know you can tell me anything. Between me and you. Nobody else. My word." Still looking directly at his friend, Bull pounded his heart firmly with his closed fist. "I got you, man. I got you."

"Not here, Bull. Look. You had breakfast yet?"

"Naw, but I know where we can get a big plate of Chow Mein for a few bucks. By my house."

"Cool," Cal agreed.

The boys were silent for the rest of the ride down Fruitvale, toward Bull's place. Soon the bus approached Lynde and the two stood to get off. Once off the bus, Bull led Cal Q across the street and into The Fortune Cookie Chinese Restaurant. Selecting a seat out of the traffic of

61

patrons and waiters, the two friends settled in for a meal and some much needed friendship.

Cal sat for a few minutes, stirring his straw around in his cup of pepsi. Bull did not push him. Finally, Cal began his story.

"I got to get some bread man. I need some serious cash." Cal paused and looked straight at Bull. "That's where I was heading. A partna of mine owes me a big favor, and I thought I could hit him up for a loan."

"What for, Q? I mean. I could let you hold onto something. Why didn't you ask?"

"I just didn't want anybody to know. I mean, what I want the money for . . ." Cal stumbled over his words now.

"Go on, homie, talk to me." Bull urged.

Cal took a sip of his pepsi and held the cup in his hands, twirling it around before he spoke. "You know the story on my folks, Bull. My old man is drinking himself crazy and my mother is going crazy trying to cope with him."

"Yeah, I know," Bull whispered. "I know."

"Well," Cal took a bite out of his spring roll and chewed a long time before he spoke again. Finally, setting his food down onto his plate, he continued.

"I'm worried about my moms, Bull. She needs me, and I just ran away and left her there to struggle with Pops, alone. I call myself being independent. But Bull, a real man wouldn't run from responsibility. I've been so busy thinking about my independence, and being free, that I didn't realize that independence carries responsibilities. I need to go home, Bull. I need money to go home."

Cal was wound up now, and he talked freely to Bull about his folks. Neither he nor Bull paid any attention to the people who moved in and about them carrying trays of food. The two were now immersed in Cal's problems.

"So, what's the secret, Cal? We all know about your folks. You told us that much the night we had the open talk session, right after JoJo came into The Home."

"That's not all. I have another reason to go home."

Cal paused and looked in the direction of the door, saying nothing for awhile.

"Get it out, man. It's alright," Bull assured him.

"Responsibility is a killer sometimes, man."

"Yeah, I know." Bull said, barely audible. "And you know what else?" His voice became suddenly loud. "Responsibility can kick butt man. Ya heard?"

Something about the look on Bull's face and his sudden change of demeanor, along with the picture that Bull's last statement formed in Cal's mind, made him laugh. In fact, Cal laughed so hard that he knocked over the remainder of his drink. "Kick butt," he laughed as he got up to get some napkins to clean up the soda.

"Check it out, homes." Cal was still laughing as he approached the table. Suddenly Cal stopped and bent over, almost touching his head to the floor.

"Gettin' ready for responsibility, man. Might as well volunteer it."

The two young men laughed so hard they could hardly finish their food.

"I thought for a minute there Q, man, you were gonna drop and moon everybody." This, from Bull, brought on a fresh round of laughter.

Cal finally finished wiping up the drink and took his seat. Just as quickly as the laughter came, it disappeared.

Absent mindedly balling up the wet paper and stuffing it into the paper cup, Cal became silent. Bull responded to the sudden change in his friend's mood with equal silence. He knew that Cal had more to tell him, and that it was not funny. The laughter had only served to release the block in him. Things that some guys could say easily, came very difficult for Cal. He was not used to letting other people hear his thoughts.

"I'm gonna be a daddy." Cal blurted out.

63

Bull stopped his hand in mid-air, as he was about to take a sip from his Mountain Dew. The movement was so abrupt, that he spilled the cold, sticky drink on his hand. He grabbed his napkin and wiped his hand clean while he listened for Cal's next statement. When Cal did not go on, Bull prompted him.

"Q, man, who. . . how. . .I mean, when?" Bull's face showed his shock.

"A girl I met just before I left home. A nice sustah that I met through a partna of mine."

Cal paused and searched Bull's face for a response.

"How do you know? Did she call you or something?"

"She told my moms."

Cal stood and pulled a crumpled letter from his pocket. Sitting again, he shoved the paper in Bull's face.

"Here it is right here. My mom wrote me this last week. I've been thinking about it non-stop, man."

Bull read the letter and handed it back to Cal.

"Can you be sure that the baby is yours, Cal, man?"

"I know, man. I know that I was the first. She's sixteen, almost seventeen now, a junior in high school. She came from a nice family. All she talked about was going away to college. I know Bull. I know her." Cal paused." We got together just before I left. Man, I didn't mean for anything to happen." He took in a deep breath and let it flow out slowly." I know it's mine, Bull.

"Just want you to be sure Q."

"I know, man. I appreciate it too. But Rhea is special. I feel bad man. I feel real bad. I might be the reason she can't go to college now. I mean, she's so smart. All she talked about was going to school to be a psychologist. She wants to get a job with some big hospital one day — make something of herself, man. One thing that I like best about Rhea, she got ambition. Now. . ." Cal just shrugged his shoulder and hung his head.

Bull made no comment about Rhea's dream to go to college. He just looked compassionately at his friend.

"I got to go home, Bull. I got to go back to Chicago. Two people need me now. Soon three. I ran away once, but I won't run away from my baby. I'll be there for him-or her. I'll get a job. I'll work hard, man. If I can't be anything else, I'll be a real father to my child."

"I know you will Q. I know you will," Bull said quietly. "And we'll get you home, man. We'll get you home."

"I won't let my child grow up missing out on his daddy. Or her daddy. Whichever, I'll be there, Bull. I mean it. I'll be there. I'll always have my baby's back." Cal shut his eyes tight and hit his clenched fist into his open palm.

"I know," was all Bull could answer.

Bull and Cal Q talked all morning. In fact, they talked so long that they both ordered a second plate of food, this time shrimp fried rice. It was about one o'clock before they got up to leave. Cal took a bus to the other side of town to find his friend to borrow money. Instead of crossing the street to his apartment, Bull headed back to the bus stop to get on the 39, going back up Fruitvale. He had decided to go straight to The Home. He could have walked the distance to Elbow's, but he felt an urgent need to take care of some unfinished business with the men.

As Bull once again settled into his seat on the back of the bus, he tossed Cal's story around in his head. He felt deeply for his buddy's situation. He didn't know the girl, Rhea, but he also felt for her.

"He's going to see his mother," Bull thought out loud. "He's going to see his mother."

Something like a hot rope knotted up in his chest and suddenly dropped to the pit of his stomach. He realized how brave Cal was being. When he thought of his own mother, he tried to summon something brave inside of himself. All he could come up with was that feeling of sand and glass, once more, sifting through his mind.

Chapter Seven

SOME UNFINISHED BUSINESS

What about that action you promised us?

Bull knew that all of the brothers would be at The Home that afternoon around two o'clock. Saturday was the day they hung around, kicking it together. But after last night's incident, he wasn't all that sure.

"Well," Bull thought as he approached the door. "Belt tightening time. A leader is a leader, and that's me." He opened the door with his key. As he expected, they were all there lounging around, just chillin' out. When Bull stepped through the door, Tailgate and Flippo stood up and headed toward him.

"Notice a change in the air here, Flip?" Tailgate threw Bull a hot-dart look.

"Yeah, man, sorta like hung-out-to-dry dead fish." Laughing sarcastically, they headed for the door.

"You in this club, you stay. You walk, you out." Bull shot back at them. "We got business to take care of."

"We had business last night," Flippo snapped. "You walked. Remember that, Mr. Leader?" On the word, "Leader," Flippo glared hard at Bull, tightened his mouth and made a spitting motion in Bull's direction. Bull ignored the insult and continued his orders.

"I'll decide what the business is around here. Now sit down." Bull snapped his finger and pointed to the sofa.

"What! You telling somebody to sit down and listen to you," Flippo growled. "You ain't got nothin' to say to me, man."

Before he could reach for the door, Elbow was behind him.

"I believe our leader gave you an order. He has something to say, and we'll all listen. Sit down, Flippo — Tailgate. Act like men, okay?"

Elbow, being next in line to Bull, believed in showing respect to position. Even when he did not agree, he insisted that orders were orders, and a leader is a leader, after all.

"We'll listen on one condition," Flippo bargained. He tossed a sneaky glance at Tailgate and nudged him knowingly. He pointed accusingly at Bull.

"That he tells us where he spends all of his time lately. You, yourself, have wondered about it Elbow. We all have. He's out of here more than he's in."

"Yeah," chimed Bop.

The room was filled with mumbling. It was clear that JoJo and Jake did not agree with Flip and Tailgate. While Jake shook his head and scowled at the boys' argument, JoJo sat sullen-faced and quiet, letting his big brown eyes roam from one agitated face to the next.

"A'ight, a'ight. What's up, chief? We got a bunch of babies here who need a sucker to calm them down. Peace — huh?" Elbow looked Bull straight in the eyes, appealing to his sense of big brotherhood.

Signaled by a wink of the eye from Elbow, Flippo and Tailgate reluctantly left the door and joined the others on the ragged linoleum floor.

"You got all the answers and all the questions," snapped Bull. But where I spend my time is not yours or anybody else's business. Forget it."

"See. See what we mean?" Tailgate shouted, jumping up abruptly. "He think' he' all that. Can't be real with us. He can give all the orders, but he can't be real." Tailgate dropped heavily back onto the floor.

"Okay. Okay. Then what about the training? What about *us*?" Bop jumped up. He dragged himself across the floor, in his usual cool fashion. "What about us?" He pounded his fists into his chest.

"So you wanna learn to fight better, huh? You want guns and knives. You want street flavor. You wanna learn to be the big dog that eats up the little dogs. That's gang talk. You wanna smoke somebody, Tailgate? Huh? Is that it?" Bull stared at Tailgate a moment and then let his eyes move to take in the whole group. "We agreed that we were not a gang, that we were brothers, holding each other up; that we..."

"Man, save it! That's all you been hollerin' these days — B.S.!" Bop lost control. "They got these streets. They got these babes. They got *us*, and all you can talk about is holding each other up. We gonna hold each other up alright Bull, but we gonna do it our way now, cause you can't seem to deliver what you promised us. We're tired of the *Be Cool* talk. It's *ACTION* time, homie! It's action time!"

By now they were all worked up. Elbow tried to keep them calm while Bull appealed to reason. There was no calm in them. There was no reasoning with them. There was only jumbled, unidentified mixture of lava boiling inside where feelings belonged, spilling all over him. All over one another.

The explosion ended with Flip and Tailgate stalking out the door. JoJo excused himself to run an errand for his father. "It's the only way to keep him from bugging me about where I go," he explained. He slipped sheepishly out the door.

"Come on, men." Bop eased over to Jake and MopMan. Let's hit the streets. We'll find our own action. If we don't feast, we'll become somebody's feast." He scowled at Bull. "You used to preach that one yourself, Bull, back in the day.

Remember? Throwing another scowl at Bull, he solicited allegiance from the others. "Come on ya'll. Let's get out of here."

Mop didn't budge. Jake stood, looking at no one in particular. He opened his mouth as if to speak, but nothing came out. He just stood in front of Bull, waiting. Bop, with more speed than usual left by himself.

Hesitating briefly, Jake questioned "You need something, Bull? I'm going down to pick up some fish sandwiches, some slaw, and a coke."

Motioning his decline with his hand, Bull dismissed Jake. Taking the hint, Jake opened the door and walked out.

Without any words, Mop raised himself from the floor and walked over to Bull. As he crossed in front of Bull, Mop simply tapped his leader's shoulder lightly with his fist and made his exit.

The silence between them was thick. Neither seemed to want to start, but Bull knew that Elbow had had all he could take for now, and that something between them had to be settled. Elbow always stood by Bull and did not question him in front of the others, but on more than one occasion he had cautioned Bull to listen more to the brothers, and push them less. Bull knew that Elbow had something he needed to clear up with him. He had seen it in Elbows eyes all through the scene with Tailgate and Flippo last night, and he was seeing it now. Bull started, "Elbow man, I . . ."

"Hey, it's cool man. . ."

"Don't give me that Bow. I appreciate how you stand by me in front of the fellas, but it's just you and me now. Talk to me, man."

Elbow stood and walked calmly over to stand full stature in front of Bull. Bull met his gaze. Raising his long thin finger and pointing to the door, Elbow spoke, almost between his teeth, slowly and deliberately.

"It's them, Bull. It's them — the young bruthas who just left here. They're puzzled — mad. It's them, man, you need to listen to them." With this Elbow took a deep breath, and let it out as he shook his head. He threw both his hands up, palms facing Bull, in surrender. "Hey, you got the answers, Bull. Give 'em to us. Just say what's on *your* mind. Everybody can see your biggest fight ain't wit' us. You ain't been the same Bull. Something is changin.' Shaking his head again and dropping his hands, he almost shouted. "Hey, I'm otta here." And he left.

Alone, Bull stood for a full five minutes, starring at the door, thinking nothing in particular, yet thinking everything all at one time. The sand and glass were beginning to sift through his mind again. He needed some relief from it all. How could he make them know what he himself didn't know yet?

Yeah, he had started working. Yeah, he had a special young woman in his life; but something was missing. Something had slowed down in him. He didn't have that head-on attack for things anymore. He was in a slump. He was just plain in a slump.

"Okay," he spoke aloud. "We'll do it. We'll throw a party. Not a big one. Wouldn't want the word to get out to the wrong cats. I promised the homies that I would do all I could to see to it that the cops didn't single this place out for trouble, and I aim to keep that promise." Bull took a deep breath and let it out in a puff.

"On the other hand," Bull continued speaking to himself. "If I keep them pinned up here, they'll just go out looking for fun. And that," he reasoned, "that would just send them right into the dark hole that I just climbed out of, the same dark hole that I'm desperate to save them from."

He paced a few feet and stood staring at the poster of Tupac, speaking directly to it.

"Man, you were just beginning to come into the light — and, WHAM, yours went out."

To himself again, Bull gave a caution. "Don't be so nervous. Just don't be so nervous. You left the gang. You didn't look back, and no one has bothered you since you proved to them that you meant business. Now relax. This is a different kind of place here with the homies. At the rate you're going, you won't even have them. Relax, dude. We gonna have some fun."

Getting excited now about his decision to throw a party, Bull pulled his cell from his hip pocket and hit Hal on speed dial. It took some begging, but he finally convinced his brother to give up his car for an hour so that he could "take care of a little business." At breakneck speed, he made his way on foot from Elbow's to his place to pick up the Tercel.

Bull knew exactly where Elbow was headed. He knew that his partner would be sitting at Lake Merritt watching people, staring at the ducks on the water, just chillin'. It was what Elbow always did when he was upset, tired or just needed space. Today was no different. Spotting Elbow on a bench by himself, he walked over to join him. Without even greeting him, Bull eased onto the bench beside his partner.

"My bad, dude, Elbow began. I shoulda stayed and talked it out."

"Naw, Bow, this one's on me. I get so. . ." Bull did not finish his thought. He just threw up his hands in exasperation.

"Look, Bull, we just probably all need a break right about now," Elbow offered.

"Like that party, huh?"

"Yeah," Elbow agreed. "Like that party."

"Okay." Bull stood abruptly, and stretched his arms wide. His whole manner and mood took a sudden change, and the grin on his face surprised Elbow.

"Okay, let's do it! Let's party Bow. I got a few slices put aside. Money ain't no thing. Let's do this."

The mood change was contagious. Laughing, Elbow stood as abruptly as Bull had.

He thrust his clenched fist through the air. "Let's do this then. Let's just do this. I'll get the word to the homies and everything'll be set up for tonight."

"Careful Elbow. This is just a small get together," Bull cautioned.

"Got'cha!" Elbow grinned, and got up to go find the others.

"Oh, Elbow. I'll go hit Q up 'bout being the DJ for the night. You do the rest."

"Got'cha," Elbow said again. "Slap me some man." Elbow raised his fist in the air. The two young men gave each other daps, closed the conversation with a chest bump, and went separate ways.

Chapter Eight

Hip-Hop The Night Away

It's time ya'll; the battle's on!

Around nine that night, the party was on. Elbow had stacked the mini refrigerator with cold beer. Hard liquor and drugs were not allowed. An occasional beer for those who could handle it was permitted. They wanted to have a party, but they didn't want trouble. And a large, hard party was nearly always trouble.

Elbow had moved things around in his humble living room to make space for a few more chairs and a couple of card tables - room for dancing.

A steady rap beat vibrated through the small house. Getting the party warmed up, three or four people moved singularly in slow hip-hop fashion to the rhythm of the late Tupac Shakur, while others sang out in unison:

> Help me raise my black nation
> Reparations are due - it's true
> Caught up in this world
> We took advantage of you . . .
> Born Black in this white man's world. . .

My man should'na gone out like that. Pac was on it," one young man in a group said.

"Won't be another like him. Pac was the realist. Style can't be compared!"

Two of the young men slapped hands in the air, moved onto the floor, and started dancing, each into his own world, executing some rather sharp hip-hop kicks and flips while others stood around clapping and warming to the beat themselves.

"Hey Q!" one young woman on the dance floor shouted, "Hit us with the baddest sustah alive. I know you got to have some Keyes – my girl, Alicia!"

"Got'cha covered girl! *You don't even know my name,* comin' up."

In Bop's own words, "The party was off the hinges – jamming." Yet it was just the way Elbow and Bull wanted it to be — fun, with no trouble. It felt cool. Everyone was having a good time. Bull had even managed to borrow some strobe lights for the occasion. The rap beat and the rapid flickering of the lights added excitement to the party. Even Tailgate and Flippo showed up. A good party was a rare thing lately. Besides, wherever the action, there was Flippo.

"Yo, Tailgate, check it out. My boy, Mr. Mop his'self, try'na hang. Hey, Mop. Don't you know white men can't dance." Flippo shouted in a taunting voice.

"Chill, Flippo," MopMan warned. "Don't make me have to handle you tonight."

"Can't take the truth," huh, Mop. And got the nerve to be try'na hip-hop wit' a sustah. Move man, let a real Brutha show you how."

Suddenly, Flippo shoved MopMan aside. Before anyone could stop it, the fight was on. MopMan landed a hard right jab into Flippo's stomach. Flippo bent over in pain for a second, and thrust the weight of his body into MopMan, pushing him against the wall. Before either man could throw another blow, both Elbow and Bull had them under control. Elbow grabbed MopMan's arm and twisted it behind his back, while Bull restrained Flippo with his arm around his neck.

"What's the matter with you, Flippo? You asked for some action, now you're gonna ruin it for everybody. The one thing we don't need around here is a fight." Bull tightened his grip on the struggling Flippo. MopMan was no longer fighting, so Elbow let him go.

"Man, chill. Don't pay Flippo no attention. He's got his own brand of problems. Just go have some fun. Elbow tapped MopMan on the shoulder with his fist."

"Yeah, Mop. Don't mind Flip. He's just what his name says, flip and crazy. Always cappin' on somebody." This came from Sandra, the girl Mop was dancing with.

"One more move like that and I'll teach him to flip out. Ya heard?" Mop took Sandra by the hand and moved back onto the floor. Soon the beat of the music distracted him from his anger. In no time he was back into his party mood and the slow easy motions of the music and the girl whose arms seem to tighten around his waist, eased him.

"If you can't do any better than this, Flippo, you gotta go. What's up, man?" Bull tried to reason with Flip. You trip when you're not having fun and you trip when you could be having fun. You just can't be peaceful, can you"

"Yeah right. So you take that white boy's word over mine, huh. Yeah, I see where you comin' from, Bull."

"I don't have anything to prove to you Flip. But you'd better leave that liquor and weed alone if you want to keep hanging out here at The Home. I can smell it all over you. You know the rules man. The last thing we need around here is a cop."

"Rules, rules. What is this, some kind of prison?"

"Naw, Flip. This is so you won't go to some kind of prison. Remember the Cause. Family, man." Elbow chimed in.

"Cause! That's all I ever hear around here. I got a Cause too homie. I got a Cause," Flippo shouted.

Elbow moved closer to Flip, his voice low and calm. "It don't have to go down like that, Brutha. We can talk, man. Somethin' eatin' at you inside, Flip. Come on. Me and you; we can talk."

Flippo threw Elbow a hard quick look. "Forget your talk, Elbow. Too much talking 'round here already."

Mumbling about talking, prison rules, and his own Causes, Flippo strutted pass MopMan who was now enjoying his dance, and was oblivious of him. He glared in Mop's direction and stalked angrily to the door.

"Hey Gate, you comin?" He shouted over the bass of a slow Maxwell sound.

Tailgate was dancing with Alethea, a pretty young woman, who had both arms around his waist. He ignored his partner's call.

"Hey Tailgate, wassup? you comin'?"

Tailgate lifted one hand behind his back and signaled Flippo to go ahead. Still clinging to Alethea, he called behind him. "Catch you later, partna. 'Sides, my man Usher gon' be in the house next. Show some respect, bruh."

"Be that way, punk," Flippo shouted at him.

Just as Flippo was about to step outside, he met his younger foster brother at the door.

"What do *you* want?" he shouted at the boy.

"Mama Sellers says for you to come home. She says you're gonna get yourself into a lot of trouble if you don't stop hangin' in the streets all the time," the younger boy said.

"She is not my mother, and that is not my home, and you can tell her I said so. Now get out of here." Flippo pushed the boy out the door.

"Hey Flip, man, chill. That's your lil' bruh. Man. you don't treat family like that." Elbow rushed to the rescue. "Wassup, lil homie?" Elbow greeted the boy.

"Wassup?" the kid greeted Elbow. "Flippo got to come home. I was told to come get him, but he won't come," the boy explained.

"It wouldn't hurt for you to go see what your folks want, Flippo. You never know. Your family might need something, man. Hey Flip — be a man. Go see what your family wants, a'ight?" Elbow reached calmly for Flippo's shoulder. Flippo knocked Elbow's hand away.

"How many times do I have to say she is not my mother and you are not my father, Elbow. Stop try'na tell me what to do. If it's not you, it's Mr. Eagle Scout over there. But I got news for both-a ya'll — especially Mr. Scout man. With this, Flippo stormed out of the door with his younger brother trotting behind him.

The others returned to the party. The music and the laughter was loud, but not blaring.

Some of the girls had brought buffalo wings and potato salad. The guys had provided chips and dip and drinks. Jake and Bop picked up the bowl of chips and the dip and began circulating the room, offering the food as they went. Of course, Bop had to offer one of his "cool" lines to any girl that wasn't with a guy. Bop's idea of flirting.

"Hey Bop, think you can leave the women alone long enough to make your way over here with them chips and dip?" Cal Q called from the DJ's corner.

"Fa' Sho, my man. Fa' Sho." Bop grinned as he moon walked himself over to Cal.

Bull, himself, was getting into the swing of the party right along with everyone else when someone shouted from the door," Hey Bull, some dude wants you at the door. Say he can't come in."

Putting down the plate of potato salad and the pepsi he had in his hands, Bull strolled to the door and walked out into the night. Standing just where the dry, dead grass meets the cracked sidewalk, slant wise from Elbow's place, was a figure that Bull knew so well. With a sudden change in attitude, he pounced on Mack.

"Mack, man, What's up with this? Why you calling me outside? Nobody inside looking to hurt you, dude." Bull was clearly annoyed with Mack's surprise visit.

In an urgent whisper, Mack started to explain.

"Bull, man, just give me some clock. Got a word or two for ya. Been thinkin'...

"Before Mack could get his words out, Bull cut him off, with a harsh wave of his hand.

"Not now, Mack. You can come in and get down with this party we got going on here for the homies, or you can hit me up some other time."

Seeing the stern look on Bull's face, Mack relented. "Ok, bruh. I got 'cha. It's like that."

Without another word, Mack turned and rushed away. Crossing over to the darker side of the street he disappeared as quickly as he had come. Shaking his head and mumbling something about lagging brothers, Bull went back in to the party.

"Ya'll better eat up tonight," Bop was shouting when Bull entered. "Cause the bruthas won't be feedin' ya'll no more after this," Bop concluded. Everybody laughed, including Bull. And the party went on.

About an hour later, when everyone was well into the party groove, Bop pimp-strolled out to the center of the floor and shouted over the music, "Everybody, listen up!"

"Wassup!" somebody yelled back.

Moving his feet in a quick criss-cross kick, Bop held up a five dollar bill for everyone to see.

"Had myself a little conference with Mr. Lincoln here. . ."

"Yeah," Elbow laughed. He knew Bop, and he knew what he was up to.

By now, Bop had everybody's attention, even Jake, who had spent the evening watching everybody dance while stuffing himself with chicken wings and potato salad. Wolfing down a hand full of Fritos, Jake turned to see Bop.

"My boy Abe here says that it's BATTLE TIME YA'LL! And I got to listen to my boy, you know. THE BATTLE'S ON!" Bop did a quick spin and landed in a split on the floor.

"One Five on the Lincoln side to whoever can get some of this." Bop spread his arms wide and did another quick spin.

"Jam some Chris Brown for starters and then I'll take whatever you got," he yelled at Cal Q.

"Don't matter what the sound is." Cal threw a taunting grin at Jake.

"THE BATTLE'S ON!" Bop was in his element and the music was pumping his blood.

A cheer went up from the party-goers. Everybody knew that Bop was the best dancer in the place. They also knew that it would be hard to find someone eager to accept his challenge to a battle. But battling was Bop's favorite way of dancing.

While Bop rocked and spinned to the music, someone suddenly grabbed Jake and pushed him out onto the floor before he could realize what was happening. Everybody finally stopped dancing. JAKE THE SPACE. This they had to see.

"Oooh, I'm scared," Bop teased Jake.

"They shouldn't do this to Jake," Sandra whispered to the girl next to her.

"Put a hurtin' on him Jake," shouted Bull. "Open up one of your books and whip him with a quote."

"Send him out to space, Jake," Elbow shouted. Everyone laughed.

"Murder that cat," someone else added.

JoJo placed his cup of punch on the radiator and took a seat on the floor beneath Cal.

"Not Jake," he called to Cal.

"Hey Jake, make like Michael Jackson and bust a moon-walk on him."

At the mention of Michael Jackson, a shout went up, and Cal Q got the message.

"Respect for the fallen King of Pop," Bop shouted.

In a second, Cal Q had "Bad" blasting at full volume.

"Put on your moon shoes, Jake, cause here I come . Take- off time." Bop began to slide across the floor in an easy backward moon walk motion and the crowd went wild.

Don't let him scare you, Jake. Discombobulate 'em Dawg." Everyone roared at Elbow's choice of words.

Jake attempted to capitalize on the laughter and make his way back to his corner.

"Gotta give Cal a hand DJ'ing," he mumbled, hoping desperately to escape this trap.

"Sounds are fine, Jake." Elbow taunted. "Cal doin' his thing just fine. You okay over there, Cal?" Cal's face showed pity for Jake but he wouldn't spoil the fun. "Sho," he yelled back at Elbow. "You been called out, Jake. Can't help you, Man."

"See man, the DJ"s just fine. Mr. Lincoln is calling your name, Jake." Bop laughed as he did a James Brown slide on one foot, waving the five-dollar bill, and then slipped easily back into his moon walk.

The beats bounced off the sheetrock wall, to the radiator and seemed to land in Bop's feet. He took off, dancing circles around Jake. He executed smooth slides. One minute he was a gazelle gliding through an open field. Next he was a whooping crane, one leg in the air and the other on the floor. Bop was waving and popping, electric boogaloo style. Bop was housin' it up and daring Jake all the while.

"Go Bop! Go Bop!" the group was ecstatic.

All of a sudden something broke loose in Jake. Like a panther after a prey, he slid on his knees, stood up, posed, and took off in a series of shakes, swaying from side to side – alternating with ticking and freezing. Jake began to twirl and glide with ease, in total control.

The gang was shocked. They couldn't believe that this was slow-moving Jake, the book worm.

"Throw some Duggie on him," Jake.

"Bring it up to date, Jake." Throw that Whip on him. Hit him with that Stanky Leg!"

" Cat Daddy that dude off the floor Space Man. You got the moves. New school, all the way."

"Hit 'em hard Jake! The cheers and laughter grew louder.

"Knock him down with the Milly Rock, Jake."

Every dance the crowd called out, Jake jumped into, executing moves around Bop, wearing a big grin like the crowd never saw on Jake's face.

"Go Jake! Go Jake!" They began to scream with excitement. The more they screamed the smoother and quicker Jake moved. While his quickness was that of a panther, he was as light on his feet as a deer gliding through an open meadow.

"Go Jake! Go Jake!" The chant was steady.

Everyone stood and made a circle around the two dancers. Both were sweating and moving in unbelievable speed and ease. When Jake did a final back flip and dropped smoothly to the floor in a perfect split, everyone cheered. At this point Bop stopped dancing and stood back with his hands stretched out at Jake.

The music stopped and they all gathered around Jake, clapping and patting him on the back. Wiping the perspiration from his face with his shirt-tail, Bop reached into his shirt pocket, brought out the five dollar bill and made an exaggerated bow of homage to Jake.

"My Dawg!" Bop grinned and pimp-strolled over to Jake. "Steady poppin' his collar. Who woulda thought. . ." He gave Jake the bill, exchanged a dap and threw his arm around the shoulder of the panting winner. "THE BATTLE IS OVA," Bop laughed!

"Next time . . ." Jake wiped perspiration as he spoke. "Next time," he panted, "talk to Mr. Hamilton . . then meet me here."

The small crowed howled with laughter.

"And Bop. . ." Jake was wound up now."

"Yeah, Jake."

Without a warning, Jake hit some fancy tap foot work, reminiscent of the famous Nicholas Brothers, stretched his right arm out in vaudeville style, and did a quick backslide.

"Grinning from ear to ear," Jake stood close in Bop's face and sang, "Quote that!"

The crowd, including Bop, howled again.

"Hey Jake," 'MopMan called, "Who we quotin' this time?"

"Mr. Bill "Bojangles" Robinson — 'his' self," Jake laughed, unlike any of them had ever seen. This was a Jake they didn't know, and everyone in the room liked what they saw.

Walking back to the food table, Jake gave Bop a mock slap upside his head.

"You a'ight Jake," Bop said, feigning a boxing jab at Jake's shoulder. "You the man!" Everyone laughed and the party went on.

Chapter Nine

THE SCHEME

Yo, We Got Our Man

It was Sunday night, about nine o'clock, the day after the party, and Flippo was still fuming. He had called Tailgate early that morning and asked him to meet him just after dark, at the coined laundry, across the street from Bull's apartment. Flippo was at the end of his rope and had decided that it was time for some drastic changes. A few weeks ago they had shared their disgust with each other about how things were going at The Home and had made a soul-to-soul pact to do something about it.

It was time to find out just what was goin' down with Mr. Hot-Shot, Big Daddy, Bull Bullins. Why he couldn't spend more time with them, and just where all of these wimpy rules and stuff were coming from. The boys had agreed that evening, as they rode the BART over to San Francisco to chill out in "The City," and hang out a while at Ripley's Believe It Or Not," that they were fed up. After having spilled their guts to each other, Tailgate and Flippo had exchanged the power shake and thrust their clenched fist through the air, agreeing that they would cover each other on whatever "came down."

"What happened to him?" Tailgate's face was an expression somewhere between sadness and anger, as he questioned Flippo. More than anyone else in the gang, Flippo and Tailgate needed to have back the Bull that they had once been so proud to call their leader. It was that or they would have to take matters into their own hands.

"Yeah," Flippo had grinned. We 'bout to put a end to all that cat's frontin'.'"

And now the time had come. The boys sat in the wash house talking quietly and watching first one, then another drift in to collect clothes from a dryer, or to start a fresh load of wash. Now and then, Flippo would get up and peer over at Bull's apartment to see if he was coming out.

"Get down," Tailgate suddenly demanded. "The door's openin'.'"

In unison, both boys leaned their heads over into their laps. Slowly and carefully, Flippo raised his head just high enough to see Hal come through the door, walk down the stairs, right passed his Tercel, and head up the street toward the bus stop.

"Ah, lil' bruh has the wheels for the night," Flippo sneered.

"How sweet," Tailgate added. It's time our man emerged. What's taking him so long. Tailgate was beginning to get a bit antsy at this point. "Maybe we oughta just try this another day, Flip. Maybe he ain't home . . . Maybe we ought to just try another ti . . ."

Before Tailgate could get the next word out of his mouth, Flippo cut him off.

"What dawg? Do I hear a cop-out coming? You ain't down with the plan no more man, huh?"

"Naw, it's not that. You know, Flip, I mean, after all, we did have a party. He might be try'na . . ."

"Try'na what?" Flippo cut in. "Tryna' pull off a big cover up — that's what. Anyway, who's side you on, Gate - huh?" Hearing his own voice grow loud, Flippo tried to calm himself.

"That party really got to you, didn't it Gate?"

"Stop jumping to conclusions. Besides, we been sittin' here over an hour. Bull could be gone already."

"That punk's in there," Flippo insisted, looking quizzically at his friend.

"We gonna blast that punk outta the water — that's what you said, Gate. We shook on it man. You havin' second thoughts? Guess that party and that sweet lookin' little honey you had with you last night got you all wound up."

"Flippo, you losin' touch man. . ."

"I'm losin' touch? You the one talkin' 'bout givin' up here tonight when we gettin' into this thing. You still down or what? You still got my back?"

Tailgate looked his friend straight in the face. "Look man, I know the difference in gettin' with a honey and gettin' down with a homie. A'ight?"

The look on Tailgate's face — the same one that Flippo had seen there that day on the BART to San Francisco — that was the look. Flippo was satisfied. This was his Ace. Yeah, Tailgate had his back.

The two conspirators committed to wait.

"We'll find out what's really going down." Tailgate spoke in a low voice. "You right; something ain't cool about this."

"What's he scared of, anyway? Must have something to hide." Flippo added, relieved to see his partner was back into the groove of their master plan.

"Yeah!" Before this night is over, we'll have Mr. Bullins' number." Tailgate was feeling the warm surge of revolution stirring quietly beneath his skin again. "Yeah," he repeated.

The two grinned. Flippo raised his fist and this time Tailgate receive his powerful dap with a grin. The plan was sealed once more. The two continued to map out how things were to go.

About 10 minutes of silence and peering and ducking passed. Suddenly Tailgate pointed toward the apartments. Instantly, both boys tugged at their cap bills and lowered their heads. They waited a few beats before slowly raising their heads.

"Hey now! One bear in the trap. Here comes our catch," Flippo sang. "Let's go!"

"Wait, let him turn the corner first. Don't want him to see us. Got a lot at stake on this little adventure tonight," Flippo advised.

"Yeah." Tailgate grinned impishly. "Wouldn't want to mess this up for nothin'."

The two spies watched Bull all but jump the four steps down to the sidewalk and hop light- heartedly into the Tercel.

"Now!" Tailgate and Flippo exhaled the word together. Tailgate pulled the bill of his blue and gold Warriors cap down into his face for good measure. Stealthily, the two emerged from the laundry and stole over to the beat up Chevy Malibu they had begged from Tailgate's cousin. Allowing Bull to get as far as the corner stop sign, Flippo pulled the Malibu out and the hunt was on. After about twenty-five minutes of trailing and dodging, turning up one street and then another, through town and a short distance on I-880, they followed Bull as he took the Broadway exit at downtown Oakland.

Flippo slowly pulled the car behind and allowed a black Lexus and a metallic blue Honda Accord to separate him and Tailgate from Bull. Soon they noticed Bull had reached the south end of Broadway, heading toward Jack London Square. Too bad they couldn't get out. Tailgate loved the waterfront with its shops and restaurants and people just strolling or just chilling. Once, his older Uncle Robert had treated him to a fancy meal at Kincaid's Bay House.

"Show you the good side of life," his uncle had boasted. It was the first and last time his uncle had taken him any-where. In fact, Tailgate didn't even know what had happened to his mother's oldest brother after that.

Gauging the flow of the traffic, Flippo kept his foot positioned at the brake, just in case he had to make a sudden stop. About five or six blocks back, the boys could hear the whistle and clang of the Amtrak train nosing its way up the middle of the street.

Hey, Flip, let's go down on Clay, down by 10th Street and see if the Ferry is in. Just to take a quick look..."

"This ain't no school field trip, Gate. You forgot what we here for," Flippo yelled. "Focus, man. Focus."

"Don't strain ya chops," Flip. I'm on it, man." With that, Tailgate became quiet, while Flippo strained to keep his eyes on the blue Tercel two cars ahead. It was not long before they saw Bull make a right turn into the parking lot of KTVU, Channel 2, T.V.

"Channel 2! Whassup with this?" Flippo exclaimed. What's this dude up to. Sellin' us out to the world?"

"Word!" Was all Tailgate had to say.

After allowing Bull time to park and get out, Flippo edged the car into a parking slot next to the Tercel.

"This too close, Flippo. He can see us."

"Not if we get down on the floor, he won't," Flippo insisted. "Besides, Bull don't even know this car." Flippo hurriedly pulled the seat level, making squatting room for himself and Tailgate. At that the two scrunched down in the front seat, calculating their next move.

"Let's wait and see." Flippo whispered, hardly able to hide the tremor of excitement in his voice.

"You crazy, Flip! If he sees us, we dead. Wait. Give him time to get in, and then we'll decide how to handle this." Suddenly, Tailgate had taken the lead.

"Okay, okay" Flip reluctantly agreed. Flippo was not use to taking orders from his buddy. But what else was there to do but wait and figure this thing out.

"Easy, Flip. Don't let him see you".

"Now, raise your head, Flip."

At Tailgate's direction, Flippo slowly eased his head up high enough to see out of the driver's window.

"He standing by the shrubbery just outside the gate," Flippo whispered as he scrunched in place again.

The two boys remained quiet and still, not sure what to do next. The security gate that surrounded the station was only a few yards from the parking lot and the concealed spies, so they had to be sure that Bull had gotten through the gate.

Carefully measuring the time, Flippo decided that they needed another look. This time, they would both get up.

"On the count of three," Flippo suggested.

Okay." Tailgate's breathing was shallow and his voice low and hoarse.

"One. One and a half. Two, Two and a half. Three! Flippo finished the count.

As soon as their heads were raised, the two boys ducked back into hiding.

Bull had not gone in. He was standing just outside the gate, with his back turned to them. A young woman was facing Bull. The two spies had raised up just in time to see her place a quick kiss on Bull lips.

"Wow! That was quick," Tailgate whispered. "He didn't even go inside."

"And who is that luscious honey with him?" Flippo let out a long artificial breath.

Bull was definitely not alone. With him was Cheri Johnston, the beautiful new love of Bull Bullins' life. Bull had told Cheri about his secret dream to become a TV cameraman the first day they met. Cheri had insisted that he apply for a part-time position as a tech assistant. A position had just opened.

The spies, hidden on the floor of the car, held their breath as they listened to the clicking of footsteps, one loud and sure, the other quick and light, like high heels on the concrete. The footsteps ceased right at the car next to the beat-up Malibu. The boys, hunkered down even tighter, could only draw in their breath and let it out. It was a comfortably warm night so they had driven with the driver's window down, and could now hear the two lovers talking. The light, energetic voice of the young woman drifted through the air and into the car, causing the two hide-a-ways to strain not to miss a word.

"It'll be a start," Cheri was saying to Bull. "You'll at least get inside the door and see for yourself what goes on."

The young lovers stood face-to-face, on the passenger side of the Tercel. They were completely oblivious to any listening ears. Their arms were locked tight around each other. Bull gently placed his finger under Cheri's chin and tilted her head gingerly. He needed desperately to hide in the love glowing in her eyes. He just had to inhale and become drunk on the just-shampooed Dark and Lovely freshness of her hair. Neither spoke for a few seconds. Being in no hurry to get into the car, the lovers lingered in their embrace, trying to make every second count. Bull and Cheri were aware of nothing but the closeness of each other.

Inside the Malibu, the two trapped intruders geared up to take note of it all. The tension had lessened and they were poised to extract whatever evidence against Bull they could get from this unexpected twist in their mission.

Cheri met Bull's eyes with her own and raised herself to receive the tender, light kiss he placed on her lips. She buried her head in his chest. They stood for a long moment. The world had dropped out of sight just for them. It was as though they stood in a vacuum where no sounds existed but that of their breathing — one breathing for the two of them. It seemed to Bull that Cheri breathed for him. He felt at peace, yielding completely to her sweetness. He could have lived a lifetime standing there, letting Cheri's breath keep him alive.

91

"Sherman," Cheri whispered. She tilted her head and brushed his ear with her lips. "Sherman, tell me it will always be this way. Promise me, Sherman. Promise me."

"Hush," was all Bull managed to return. But in his head, unspoken, were the real words. "Hush, girl, you can't talk with that precious breath and keep me alive with it at the same time."

He gave her a long and desperate embrace, holding her tighter. He didn't ever want to be without her. But something deep inside prevented him from making the promise she begged for. He couldn't — not yet. Things had to be settled — his mother, the homeboys, his brother. She wanted him to leave The Home, to quit right away. She thought he should try to get the brothers to go back to their own homes.

There it was again, that nagging in the pit of his stomach. It struck him like a sudden fist jab in the ribs. Again he felt the scratchy glass- in-sand feeling. Again it all sifted through his mind. The pain had returned.

"Don't fight it Sherman." Cheri suddenly pulled back from him. The unexpected movement startled him, and he clutched her abruptly and clung to her. He was afraid she might run from him. She let him cling for a few seconds then pulled away from him once more. This time he did not reclaim the embrace. He simply took both her hands in both of his and held them as though his life depended on touching her.

"You don't understand, Cheri. I know what you want. I can't give you a promise. I can only promise myself one day at a time. The brothers are like family. . ."

"You have your brother, Hal," she cut in.

"The brothers are the Cause. I can't let them down." He dropped her hands and took a few steps away from her, toward the front of the car.

"What about school?" She raised her voice a half octave as he stood with his back to her. "You told me yourself if you ever decided to do something for Sherman, you would go back to school. Remember the game we played when we met? What's your dream?" Cheri was determined to make him see.

"It was a game, Cheri. Bull turned abruptly and almost ran back to her." Just a crazy game," he said softly. Once again he grab her hands as though desperate to keep her near.

"It was the truth, Sherman Bullins. And you know it. You allowed yourself one quick look inside and saw the real truth. But it was the truth."

"Okay." He stood staring out at space, feeling a sudden coldness in the air. He shivered, and again took her in his arms and held her there.

"Okay, so it wasn't just a game." Now a calmness settled over him once more. "You got me down. I'll admit. I do think a lot about going back to school. But it's not that easy. My brother. . . Kebo, - Jay… my brother." he stopped short.

Cheri wrapped her arms tighter around him and they stood in full embrace. "What about your brother?" She urged him on.

"Jay." Bull stated again and clammed up. "Jay, my brother, he was the Cause. There on the street. Shot down in cold blood by a cop who was well trained to see all black folks looking alike. I swore that I'd do all I could to see to it that brothers learned to protect themselves from the cops, that they had friends to count on and that . . ."

"Sherman, can't you see? That's every reason to quit completely now. You told me your brother was in a gang. It didn't work that way. It never does, my sweet man. It never does."

She was looking up at him, her eyes pleading. He couldn't stand to look at her just now. She was too warm, too real, too pleading. He mustn't give in to her. He suddenly felt like running. He wanted to run without any regard to where he was going. He just wanted to lift one foot fast in front of the other and pass through the air at bullet speed. He wanted to work up a sweat and fall out on the ground and stay there.

Mesmerized, locked in Cheri's cinnamon glow, he could not move. He was held in place by the deepness of her eyes, by her lips and her dimple. Her voice stirred him to panic one minute and soothed him to a safety zone the next. Holding her even closer, he allowed her voice to lull him to calmness.

"Sherman, look at you. Do you know what I see when I look at you and then listen to you talk about your Cause and the brothers' need for you?" She stood back from him and cocked her head, looking up at him. "I see a kind, compassionate, warm guy trying hard to live up to other people's hard image of him."

Inside the other car, in the half-dark, a sarcastic scowl passed over Flippo's face, but neither spy dared whisper a word. It was late, and there was little honking of horns, few motors starting up, and hardly anybody passing by. The only noticeable sound was the voices of the couple totally immersed in a sweet and crucial moment.

Still looking in his face, Cheri continued." I see a confused, sweet loving guy trapped in a Cause that is not his, but someone else's for him. I see a young man with all kinds of potential to be a real brother, an educated man, one with the skills and resources to really keep young men off the streets. Sherman, my sweet, beautiful black man, educated, you could make a real difference.

"And what about your dad," Bull abruptly thrust her away, and held her at arm's length

"What about my dad? What does he have to do with any of this." She was a bit startled by his abrupt reference to her dad.

"It's no secret that he hates the sight of me, Cheri. Even you know that. You told me yourself that your father believes that every dropout has a criminal record and could never amount to anything,"

"Yes, but he hasn't had a chance to get to know you, Sherman. In fact, he only saw you briefly, once, and that was..."

"Yeah," he cut in. I know what that was. Your dad chewed me up in a split second and spit me out right there in his own front yard."

Feeling a sudden annoyance with him, Cheri moved out of his arms and stepped back to look directly at him. "I told you how sorry I was for what my daddy did to you Sherman. And I am. I really am."

"Cher. . ." His tone was tender again. He didn't finish, but Cheri could see the tension in his face. She knew how badly Bull wanted to clean up his past image and be appreciated for what he was becoming. Yet she also knew that it would take time. Sherman Bullins was on the right track, doing just that – changing. The pain in his gentle, dark, brown eyes grasped her heart. Moving toward him, she embraced him and tucked her head under his chin.

"Sherman or the Bull," she whispered again. "Which?"

He didn't answer. He just let her head rest there on his chest, wishing now that he could breath for the two of them. Quietly, he pulled her closer to him and held her in a calming embrace. Without saying a word, he finally released her and opened the car door for her to climb in. Once Cheri was settled in her seat, Bull walked around the back of his car to the driver's side. Without saying another word, he opened his door, got in and drove away.

Like two swimmers who had been holding their breath under water for a long time, Flippo and Tailgate popped their heads up from their place on the car floor. When they saw that Bull had driven out of sight, Flippo jumped out of the car, with Tailgate following after him.

"Yo! We got our man!" The two partners hopped about like pee wee baseball players after a first win, slapping each other against the hands. They had triumphed! They had succeeded in their mission to get some destructive information against Bull.

It was sheer luck, they knew, but it was real. Never would they have imagined such a perfect setup for their plan.

Suddenly, Tailgate stopped jumping. A pensive look spread slowly across his face.

"Hey, who died?" Flippo asked.

"I don't know, Flip. I wonder if we shoulda' . . ."

"Hey – Hey – Hey – Tailgate. Are you letting go this victory already, man? You saw. You heard."

"That's right. I heard. He spoke up for us, man. He said some pretty cool stuff about us," Tailgate protested.

Flippo positioned himself directly in front of Tailgate, and gave his shoulder a firm punch with his fist. "Wake up, Gate, Man. That was all a hype. Bull is trying to wiggle out on his honey, just like he's doing us. Besides, she's the reason we don't get no action."

Punching both of Tailgate's shoulder's at the same time, Flippo continued his argument. "Check it out, Gate. Our honorable leader, Mr. Bull – or Sherr-man" He exaggerated the pronunciation of Bull's real name. "Mr. Sherman - alias, Bull Bullins, is getting his head filled with some mighty heavy anti-Cause junk. You heard her, Gate."

Finished with his speech, Flippo nudged his friend in the side with his fist, this time playfully. "A'ight?" He searched Tailgate's face for the right answer. Tailgate looked long and hard at Flippo and then forced a broad grin across his face.

"Yeah, man. I'm back. Yeah."

"Did we get our man, then, Tailgate?"

"Yeah, right," Tailgate answered, trying hard to feel convinced. "We got our man."

Stuffing his hands into his pockets, Tailgate dragged himself back inside the car, allowing Flippo his moment of triumph.

Chapter Ten

THE CAUSE

That low-down, two-timing liar

An hour later, Tailgate and Flippo sat in a Taco Bell wolfing down burritos and pepsis and indulging themselves in their victory.

"Head Honcho – Numero Uno, your next Home commander – General Tailgate, Suh." Flippo snickered through his words and gave Tailgate a mock salute. They both laughed and slapped each other a dap.

"Yeah, Mr. Down-With-The-Homies. No wonder our leader can't find time for us. He got a real babe – a serious lady." Flippo grunted.

"Yeah," Tailgate answered, having regained his previous, "get Bull" mindset. "A real conflict of interest if you ask me. But…" He continued stuffing bites of burrito into his mouth and mumbling through it. "But, Flip, you gotta give it to ole' Bull; our man can pick'em. You know what I mean."

The two whistled and slapped hands again. "Fine, classy sustah," Flippo laughed. "But that don't give him a right to string us along like he did. Mr. Shurrr-man, a.k.a, Bull Bullins. Lying, fake!" The two conspirators finished their meal and got up to leave. All of a sudden an idea grabbed Flippo. His abrupt halt at the door caused Tailgate to slam into him.

"Wassup, man? Why you trippin'?"

"Hey, Tailgate, you in a hurry, dawg? We got to take a ride."

"Naw, I ain't got nowhere to go. I"m down for the ride, but where we goin'?"

"Got one more mission to complete tonight."

"Where to?" Tailgate questioned.

"The James Bond action ain't over yet. Two party mamas over on Castro, over on the west side. One Yolanda McGee and one Nicole Jenkins. Got some questions for them. Got to finish this thing, homie."

"Wait a minute man. Nicole was Bull's. . ." Tailgate stopped, mouth opened, right in the middle of his sentence. "Naw Flip. I know we got a serious mission, but you fixin' to mess with Bull's woman. I know she's his ex, but Flip, man, I don't know."

"You scared?" Flippo demanded to know.

"Scared?" Tailgate dug frantically in his pants pocket and brought out a hand full of change and four crumpled one dollar bills. "Here! By the looks of that gas tank when we left our first mission, as you call it, we might end up pushing my cousin's bucket back to him tonight. Now hit me wit' the plan," he said, as he placed the money into Flippo's opened hand.

"Com' on, I'll tell you on the way. The newly acquired news about Bull had Flippo in an elevated stage of excitement and Tailgate caught between dread and excitement. The two were locked in the intrigue of their own devices. Giddy with mischief, the boys hopped into the car. Flippo took the wheel and Tailgate jumped into the passenger side and fastened his seatbelt.

"The plan, man, the plan." Tailgate insisted.

"Trust me, my man. Trust me. Got myself a funny feelin'. A real funny feelin'." Flippo adjusted himself under the wheel and clicked his seatbelt fastened.

"You see," he continued, we just found out that Mr. Cool commander is a fake. Right? He got a real gig, makin' some real bread, while the rest of us survive on Elbow's bologna sandwiches, waitin' for our leader to move us to the next level. You hear me, man?"

Whoa! Hey, learn how to drive." Flippo shouted at the driver of a white Lexus that cut in front of him too suddenly.

"Anyway," he returned to his unfinished sentence. "Anyway that cat is actually working on a normal job. You feel me? Probably got a nice education fund started in some bank. See, our man wants an E D U C A T I O N." Flippo dragged the word out sarcastically. "And that ain't all. He got himself a sweet, educated, cinnamon colored, curly-headed sustah who wants him to become educated like she is. And he wants to do this thing. Right? Check it out – a woman, a gig, and education. Does this sound like true street material? Huh? Think, Gate."

"Yeah, yeah! Go ahead." Tailgate was impatient. "So what now?"

"Well, if our leader is fake in all these areas – 1, 2, 3 – what else is Mr. Bull Bullins fakin'? Think about it. It'll hit you before we hit Castro Street."

About fifteen minutes later, close to 10:00 p.m., Flippo and Tailgate walked up the sidewalk that led to the apartment that Nicole and Yolanda shared. Without hesitation, Flippo began ascending the narrow concrete stairs that led to the second level. He had a friend who once lived in the beige and green trimmed building, close to where the girls lived. He knew it well.

Both girls had graduated from school the year before and had jobs. Together they managed the rent. Yolanda was a waitress at Denny's restaurant, and attended Contra Costa College in the evenings. Nicole was a clerk with the county. She had postponed furthering her education in order to earn money for college. Nicole and Bull had been tight for about a year. She was the only girl that Bull had spent that much time with. Though they stopped seeing each other, there didn't seem to be any hard feelings between them.

Flippo rang the doorbell of the apartment and waited.

"Just follow my lead," Flippo instructed, an evil excitement in his voice.

"Yeah. Okay." Tailgate's voice trembled. He tried not to show how nervous he really was.

The door opened, and Nicole appeared, wearing sweats with rollers in her hair. She peered cautiously at the two.

"Hi Nickie. Remember me? Flip, ah, Dante. Dante Lewis – from The Home, ah, I mean from McClymonds. I mean, I used to go . . ."

"Oh yeah," she cut in. "Bull's partna, from the MacArthur side. Yeah."

"And Tailgate – ah, Jorge Lopez, a buddy of Bull's too. Remember?" Tailgate shifted from foot-to-foot, stretching his hands deep into his pockets.

"Yeah. What are you two doing here this time of night?"

"Ah, Nicole, ah, mind if we come in a minute? We know it's late, but well, we got a little business we'd like to discuss with you. Sorry about how late it is and all. But . ."

"It is late. And some folks do work ya' know. But hey, come on in."

The guys followed Nicole into the living room where she beckoned them to sit.

"Yolanda still at work. The girl's got a real slave driver. When we decided to share this place, she started working like she gotta pay all the rent. I believe in making bucks, but there's a limit. Every time they want somebody to work overtime, they know who they can get. Oh well, that's her story. Now what's yours?" Nicole propped her right hand deliberately on her hip and set her stare on Flippo.

She noticed Tailgate staring at the five by seven color photo of her and Bull that set on a table near the door. In the photo Bull was sitting on Nicole's steps and she was perched on his leg with both her arms around his neck. It was a happy picture. Both she and Bull were laughing, and seemed very much into each other.

102

"Good ole days," Nicole volunteered, and turned her attention to Flippo, who stood eager as a puppy waiting to get to a bowl of Puppy Chow.

"What's up, Dante? I don't have much time. It *is* late, and tomorrow *is* a work day, you know."

Before answering, Flippo quickly took in the surroundings, noticing that Nicole and Yolanda had some pretty cool stuff in their small apartment. He especially noticed the brown leather sectional that filled one wall, with the smaller section arranged at the end of the adjacent wall. He noted the huge pillows, covered with gold, red, and earth tone African print, each highlighting a safari animal. His eyes quickly fell on the twenty-five inch flat screen television hinged on the wall opposite the sofa. For a moment, he seemed to have lost himself as he quietly admired the apartment.

"Hello in there." Nicole waved her hand in front of Flippo's face. "Remember me. I live here."

"Ah, nice stuff," Flippo began. Ah, hey, Nicole, you remember The Home, don't you?"

"How could I forget? That's all Bull ever talked about when he first got out of the Whips. He ate The Home in his Big Mac and drank it down in his pepsi. It was about then that we finally broke up. What about The Home?"

"Well, actually," Flippo went on, "it's not actually business. I guess business is the wrong word. Wouldn't you say so Gate?"

"Yeah!" Tailgate eased himself down onto the sofa Nicole had offered them. Flippo took the recliner across from him, and Nicole stood, resting her head against the wall, arms folded.

"Yeah, well, we hesitate to ask. I mean, I know Yolanda isn't home and you probably can't speak for her, but we were wondering, Tailgate and I, if you two would come to a jam at The Home next week. At Elbow's place, that is. It's just a little get-together. You know, with some old friends and all." Flippo paused. He shifted his eyes from Nicole to the floor and back to Nicole.

"But, ah," he paused again. "But, well, we figured what with all the talk Bull did after you two split up, well maybe you wouldn't want to come around, so . . ."

"All what talk?" Nicole took a few steps toward him. "Just what talk you speaking about, Dante?" She insisted on calling him by his real name. Placing her hands defiantly on her hips, she glared at Flippo.

By now Tailgate had the complete picture. He knew which course Flippo was taking. And he knew it was all a lie, but he was beginning to get into it now.

"Oh, we thought you knew." He chimed in. "We don't mean to start nothin' here. We figured it was water under the bridge for you two by now."

"What water? Under what bridge?" Pressing her hands deeper into her hips, Nicole threw back her head and demanded, "what water? Stop the word games, Dante. Talk!" Nicole had taken the bait off the hook and was ready to chew.

Flippo stood as though to leave. Tailgate followed his lead and stood. "Hey Nicole, we didn't mean to come here starting nothin', girl." Tailgate feigned innocence.

"Look here, Dante, and you too Jorge. You came all the way over here this time of night. You opened up a can of worms. Now don't try to put the lid back on, cause they already crawling out. So just finish this mess." Nicole's anger showed in her eyes and in the way she threw her head when she talked.

The two guys sat. Nicole remained standing.

"Well, I hate to say this," Flippo continued. "But when you and Bull broke up, the brothers got nosey and started prying, trying to find out what happened. What with you and Bull being so tight and all. Well one night we had this beer bust and well, you know better than we do that Bull just ain't no drinkin' man. Well, he did take in a couple of cold ones that night. He got to runnin' his mouth about you and one or two of his other chicks, ah ladies. Somebody asked him why you two broke up and well. . ."

"Well what?" Nicole demanded.

"Well, this ain't easy. I mean, we didn't come over here to get into you and Bull's business. We came to invite some old friends to a party. You see. . ."

"Finish Dante, or forget the party." Nicole was fuming by now.

"Well, if I gotta, I gotta." Flippo shrugged and continued.

"Bull said that night... Now check it out, he had a good beer buzz, and well. . . anyway he said that he had to let you go because you just didn't challenge him no more."

Nicole moved closer to Flippo. "What kind of challenge, Dante?"

Tailgate took over. "You know. Challenge as a woman."

"As a woman, how?" Impatient, Nicole's voice was now a good half octave higher than when they first started their conversation.

Flippo went on. "He said that you were easy. He said that he didn't even have to ask. You had started throwin' yourself at him. Said he had to get another woman, one that... I think the word was, *intrigued* him more." Flippo let the word slide around in his mouth before he spat it out in Nicole's face.

For a full fifteen minutes, non-stop, Flippo filled Nicole's head with images of an unfaithful, crude, ex-boyfriend. The more the girl twisted her face in disbelief and sucked in hot air, the wilder and meaner Flippo painted the image of Bull Bullins.

By now Nicole was pacing the floor. "That sorry, wanna-be playa'." All of a sudden Nicole stopped pacing and became quiet. She stared suspiciously at Flippo, and then at Tailgate. "How do I know you two aren't just making this up. Just to get at Bull, or something? How do I know?"

For a while the distressed young woman struggled to find some defense of the Bull she knew, the Bull whose knee she sat on in the photo, who was kinder to her than any guy had ever been. But she just couldn't pull it off. Flippo's words were sharper than any memory of Bull could be right now.

"Hey, Nicole, I know how you must feel, and, Bull is our leader. You know. We didn't come over here to talk some kiss-and-tell stuff between you and Bull. Like I said, we came over here because Tailgate and me remembered you and Yolanda as some cool sustahs. We thought you might enjoy a good jam. Ya know."

Flippo had the hooks in now, and he had no intentions of letting his prey off. In fact, he planned to turn his hooks deep into Nicole's mind. He continued to spin his web of unfaithful Bull Bullins tales until poor Nicole gave up all faith in Bull.

"Lying punk! Pretending all that time to be such a nice, thoughtful, understanding guy. Well, I'll fix him." Nicole spun around on her heels and crossed the room as though she had seen something coming after her. Abruptly she brought her full attention back to her intruding guests.

"I'll fix that punk. If talk is what he wants, talk is what he'll get. You boys want to hear a real story. Check this."

Flippo threw a knowing glance at Tailgate and worked hard to keep a grin off his face.

"For one solid year I dated Bull Bullins," Nicole began.

"For one whole year, Mr. Lover Boy, big time playa' and street gansta' did nothing more than hold my hand and give me a few hot kisses. Your idol, the woman's man, is straight up square. He's an altar boy, a baby face boy scout. Mr. Bull Sherman Bullins is a VIRGIN!" She dragged the word out as though it were the lowest word she could think to call him. It was a word meant to hurt someone she believed had said something to hurt her. Now the truth was out. They could make of it what they would.

Again the shocked young woman began pacing the floor. Breathing heavily and rapidly and waving her hands in the air, Nicole seemed to have forgotten the boys who brought this new troubled moment into her life. Flippo and Tailgate looked at her, almost fearfully. Surely, the girl was about to lose her mind.

Tailgate jumped up and ran pacing behind her. Every time he tried to reach for her, Nicole took her clenched fist and swung it at his head. Finally Tailgate gave up and sat down. He followed her with his eyes as she fanatically circled the room, calling Bull every horrible name she could think of.

"Flip, do su'm Dude. This girl's about to lose it. Say su'm to her. She losin' it."

Flippo jumped up, not as calm as he was earlier, but not as upset as Tailgate either.

"Hey, Nicole, look, it ain't that bad. I mean, everybody gets dissed sometime or another. You just got to know how to handle . ."

POW! Before Flippo knew what had hit him, Nicole's balled fist had left a red print on the left side of his face.

"Crazy woman!" Flippo drew back to deck Nicole, but his blow was intercepted by Tailgate, who pulled him away from her. As the two boys backed away and sat on the sofa, Nicole suddenly began sobbing. Tears ran down her face like water from a dripping faucet. Her sobs began loud and increased to a heavy, anguished scream. Flippo and Tailgate were bewildered. They hadn't expected this reaction from Nicole. Flippo had just wanted to make her angry enough to spill some information they could use against Bull. He hadn't dreamed that what Nicole would tell them would be so heavy or that she would go crazy on them.

Just as suddenly as she had begun, the devastated Nicole stopped crying. Tailgate and Flippo sat still, watching her as she fought to end her weeping. She struggled to even out her breath, saying nothing to them for a while. Her wet, tensed face was still. First she stared at Flippo who sat nursing his face with one hand and thumping on his leg with the other. Gradually and steadily, she shifted her eyes to Tailgate, who sat close to Flippo, almost holding his breath, not knowing whether to breathe. Nicole spoke in a slow, controlled, even voice.

"Okay. You got your story." Her pain was spent. She suddenly felt very tired, very heavy. She needed to be alone. She stared coldly at the two. When she spoke again her voice shook icicles to the floor.

"You got your story," she repeated. "Now if you'll excuse me. I have a boss to meet in the morning, bright and early." She was angry. She was hurt. She just wanted these two out of her sight. They had strolled into her life from out of the past and had robbed her of some precious, loving memories of someone who had been special. They had taken the beautiful trust of the only guy she had felt safe and warm with in her entire life.

One quick, unexpected visit, and they had stolen a hunk of sweetness from her life, and left her with a bitter ache in her bosom. Slowly, with a calculated pace, she walked over to the photo of her and Bull, picked it up, glared at it, and tossed it against the wall, where the glass shattered in as many pieces as her heart had in just one hour.

"Look, Nicole, we . . . well." Tailgate began.

"Out. . . out. . . get out of my house." She spat the words out in their faces.

"Out!" She pointed them toward the door, followed

108

them to it, and once they had charged through it, she slammed the door behind them.

Out in the street, Flippo leaped into the air and swung his hand at Tailgate for a powerful dap. Tailgate did not return it. He stood for a moment, lost in a private thought. Tailgate looked as though he wanted to cry.

"Hey Gate. Enjoy the taste of victory, man. Ain't it sweet?"

He stopped dead in the middle of his sentence when he saw the hurt look on Tailgate's face.

Suddenly, Flippo broke out in a loud laugh. "Ain't never made it with a chick. Hot kisses." Flippo gave another loud, mean laugh. "I knew it! I knew it! Hey Gate, man, it's you and me. It's Elbow, you and me. When we tell the fellas this story. . . Tailgate, hey we just won a battle and you standing out here like Jake, tripping out to space."

"I don't know, Flippo. That was a nice sustah. She was so hurt. Got so mad. Man we didn't want to invite her anywhere. Bull ain't never told us nothing about her." Tailgate paused and stared off in the direction of the apartment, then back at Flippo. "Man, she didn't do a thing to us. We left one upset sustah back there. And she's cute too, you know, Flip."

Flippo suddenly became quiet. "Hey . . . yeah man. She is a pretty nice honey, but we can't forget the Cause. Anyway, as you can see, innocent people sometimes get hurt. That's life. Remember: *You either feast or you become a feast.* Come on, man, we in the champion's corner. We hold our winning hand until the big moment comes. Then BUYACA! Mr. Bull Bullins won't know what hit'em. Right, Tailgate? For the Cause, huh?" He held his hand up for his buddy to slap. Slowly, with no enthusiasm, Tailgate tapped Flippo's fist with his fist.

Seeing the haunting look on Tailgate's face, Flippo's face dropped, right along with his hand.

"Man, Gate, I ain't never seen you like this." Flippo moved around to stand squarely in front of his friend and waved his hand in Tailgate's face. "Tailgate, man- come out of it. You forgot the Cause man. Our Cause."

Still not getting the response he wanted, Flippo grabbed Tailgate by one shoulder. "Our Cause, buddy. Hey, we tried it Bull's way. Okay, Gate?"

Tailgate took a deep breath, and let the air push deep down inside his guts to force up the words that Flippo wanted to hear.

"The Cause." Tailgate gave a half-hearted grin, and the two buddies walked silently toward the car. Tailgate walked a few paces ahead of his friend. He needed some space.

Chapter Eleven

TROUBLE AT LAKE MERRIT

This is wrong. This is dead wrong

It was about three on a nice spring, Monday afternoon, ten days after the party. Elbow had worked every day since. Mr. Green, the, manager of Grand Lake Theater, had needed him more than ever. The other janitor was sick and Elbow was the only one available. "We're in the money," he'd said when Bop asked if he had robbed Food Max. The cabinet and the refrigerator were filled, and two nights ago, Elbow had sprung for Round Table Pizza for everybody. Needless to say, Elbow felt good about being able to provide so generously for the others. Since his old '92 black Maxima was parked in front of the house waiting for a new starter, Elbow decided to walk the mile or so from the theater to Lake Merritt. He didn't think he'd ever lose his love for the lake. Next to the Oakland Bridge, it was one of his favorite places in the Bay Area.

The still, sun-glistened water and the drone of voices gave Elbow a feeling of peace and contentment. He loved the homeboys and his place was a refuge for them, just as he wanted it to be. But the Lake was his outdoor sanity spot, as he liked to call it.

He never talked much about it, but Elbow loved nature, and today was a triple reward. He felt as though he had spun the Wheel of Fortune, and the needle had landed on his number. Not only did he have money in his pocket, and not only were the guys at The Home more settled these days since the party, but he was sitting here in his favorite place, on a beautiful spring day, feeling good all over.

Elbow closed his eyes and let the sounds nurture his spirit. A distant drum beat caught his attention and he subconsciously rolled his head to the music. From one corner near the gazebo he could hear a mother softly scolding a child who had run out of her reach toward the busy street. Opening his eyes, Elbow watched with a particular interest as the mother lifted the child, his brown legs kicking in protest. He kept his eyes on them until the mother and child headed in the direction of Fairyland.

On the other side of him, Elbow could hear a homeless man repeating the words," some spare change." Digging into his pocket, he pulled out three quarters and a crumpled dollar bill and made his way over to the homeless man sitting on a bench with his hand out toward anyone who would drop something in it. The only words exchanged between the two as Elbow placed the money in the man's hand, was a gruff, but appreciative," Cool, thanks cat," from the receiver. Elbow gave a knowing smile and returned to his own seat. Settling again into the sounds and sights of the lake area, he gave himself completely to his sanity time.

The repeated swishing of car tires up and down the busy street behind him, kept a steady rhythm, interspersed with the honking of horns and an occasional screech of a brake. From out in the middle of the lake from where Elbow sat, he could hear the call of the driver of one paddle boat to someone in a second boat. The two seemed to be in some sort of race to get to the other side.

All of these sounds were familiar to Elbow. He had heard so much of the pain of his city, yet, this area at Lake Shore Avenue and Grand Avenue, in Oakland, was balm to his often-troubled mind. Neither the wail of the siren nor the police car at his back could disturb him. He sensed nothing horrendous in their call this afternoon.

"And who you two dudes," Elbow chuckled focusing his attention on two pigeons that seemed to recognize him.

These two made their way to where he sat. They stood directly in front of him, as though they knew that he would feed them. When Elbow stood to find food for them, the pigeons, questioning their own judgment, waddled away.

"So, be that way," Elbow admonished them. "Y'all know me. Did I ever do you any harm?" Spotting a corner of bread near a trash can, Elbow walked over and picked up lunch for his friends. Just as he returned to his spot on the bench, the birds, with three or four other friends and family members, returned.

"I knew you'd come back." Smiling at the birds, Elbow broke the piece of bread into several pieces, and tossed it out to them. "Yeah, you know a real partna when you see one."

"Hey, Elbow. Wassup!"

He turned his head quickly to see JoJo bouncing toward him, eyes squinting as he jog-walked over to Elbow. In a playful, bunnyhop, JoJo landed directly in front of Elbow.

"Sup, Elbow"

"Ain't nothin', lil' homie. You the one. School out?"

"I guess so." JoJo shrugged his shoulders.

"Now what's that suppose to mean? 'I guess so.' Anybody who's been in school all day ought to know if school is out – wouldn't you say, lil' homie."

"Yeah, anybody who went to school oughta know." JoJo took a seat next to Elbow.

"Whatcha' doin' sittin' here? You gotta work today?"

"Whoa! Back up, dude. This conversation ain't 'bout me and my work. This is 'bout you and whether or not you went to school today," Elbow spoke, almost sternly.

JoJo took a deep breath and let it out. He said nothing.

Elbow turned himself around fully to look JoJo directly in the face. "Sounds like a little probing is in order here. I take it your teachers didn't see you again today." Elbow didn't wait for an answer from JoJo.

"What did we talk about just last week, JoJo? And what

did you promise both Bull and me you would do for two weeks non-stop?"

"Ah, Bow man, I tried, but ain't nothin' hap'nin in school. Teachers talking about junk that just a few nerds know about, and . . ."

"JoJo, did it ever occur to you that if you went to class enough you would know what the teachers and the nerds, as you call them, are talkin' 'bout."

"Come on, Elbow, I stayed in school longer than you. Anyway, the only person in The Home who finished school is Jake. So why come y'all always on my case? Huh?"

Elbow turned again and stared at JoJo before he spoke. "So, you gotta go there, huh?" Everybody else blew it so now it's JoJo's time to blow it. Well listen to me and listen good, lil' brutha." You want some reasons for stayin' in school. I'll give you some. One – to stay out of jail. Two – to get a better job than sweeping popcorn from the floor of a theater and unsticking gum from underneath the seats. Three – a wife and some children." Elbow paused and listened for JoJo's response. Hearing none, he continued.

"For number four, how about just feelin' good about JoJo, and five, just to *learn* a lil' su'm, su'm. Is this enough *why comes* for ya?"

"You wanna know the truth, Elbow? I don't need none of that. I got my own thing goin'."

Before JoJo could finish his sentence, Elbow stood up and began walking away from him, in the direction, heading out toward Grand Avenue.

"Hey Elbow – where you goin' man? Elbow wait up." JoJo jumped up and ran behind Elbow, who said nothing to him. Elbow walked in silence. When JoJo realized that his older friend would not talk to him, he too walked in silence.

Elbow walked at a fast pace with his hands locked behind his back, while JoJo increased his pace. Suddenly, Elbow began a low whistle. JoJo didn't recognize the tune, but he had heard Elbow whistle it before. In fact, he had heard it when Elbow was upset and didn't want to talk.

"Bow, you mad?" JoJo asked, almost apologetically. "You mad, man?"

The older friend did not answer. He just kept his stride. When he reached the curb, he stopped, with several other pedestrians, to wait for the light to change to "Walk." JoJo finally caught up to him at the curb.

Just as the "walk" signal appeared, and Elbow was about to step from the curb, a police car with its siren wailing, turned in and stopped right in front of the group about to cross. Elbow, JoJo, and the other pedestrians attempted to walk around the car. At this time, a second car pulled up to the curb behind the first. There was one officer in each car.

Before anyone could assess the situation, the police officers, a white male and a black female, jumped from their cars and rushed toward the small crowd. The male officer pounced on Elbow, pinning his arm behind him and cuffing him, while the second officer, a woman. did the same to JoJo, as she hurriedly recited their rights to them.

"Wassup officer? We didn't do nothin' wrong." Elbow twisted his head around to see the man arresting him ." This is wrong. This is dead wrong," Elbow insisted.

"Shut up," the cop demanded, as he twisted Elbow's arm hard enough to cause Elbow to grunt in pain. "You'll get a chance to prove if this is wrong or not. In the meantime, you and your little buddy here will be taking a ride down town."

"He's only fourteen and he didn't..." Another twist of his arm from the officer didn't stop Elbow's plea for JoJo. This time, he refused to let the officer see how much pain he was in.

"I'm tellin' you, y'all got the wrong ones," Elbow managed to rush the words out. This time the officer placed his right hand on the top of his holstered gun, while giving Elbow's arm one more extremely hard jerk. Elbow could not help but grimace in pain.

After searching both, they shoved Elbow into one car and JoJo into the other. When Elbow and JoJo were united at the precinct, Elbow could tell that JoJo had been crying. Of course, he was scared. This was his first arrest.

Chapter Twelve

BEHIND BARS

I don't belong here. I just don't belong here

At the precinct, the two were reunited during the processing period.

"You'll be alright lil' brutha," Elbow assured the younger boy. "You'll be out of here in no time."

JoJo tried to smile, but he was too scared to even fake it.

After about an hour of questioning, Elbow was allowed to make a call. He contacted Bull, who arrived in just under thirty minutes. After another hour, in which both Elbow and JoJo were put through a tougher battery of questions, JoJo was released to his father, and Elbow was booked on suspicion of armed robbery.

"Here we go again. A brutha just can't get past it, Bull. If I sit by the Lake feeding pigeons, I'm doomed. If I rob somebody, I'm doomed. What's the point man? What is the point?"

Elbow's pain was deep, and Bull had no answers. The truth of his friend's words set heavy in front of him. All he could manage to say was, "We'll raise some bail, Elbow. We'll get you out of here, man. You can count on it."

Once again, it was a long, chilling walk for Elbow. He had never intended to go this way again. He had worked hard, living almost in squalor, taking menial jobs, and avoiding confrontation – all this to keep from having to take this walk again.

As he went passed the long row of cells, he feared that the sudden lightness in his head would cause him to fall. The clinking of the jailer's keys just made it worse. On one hand he would like to have fainted to escape the feeling. At the same time, he needed to be aware of what was happening. Jail is no place to zone out. A man needed to be aware of his space at all times.

Something inside of him locked up when the attendant slammed the cell door and Elbow was once more behind bars. He fought to drown out the clanging of iron on iron as the cell door had been slammed behind him.

"Trapped," he thought. "They might as well strip me naked, from head to feet, stand me in front of everyone here, and beat me. That would have more dignity to it than this." Elbow tried not to look around. He tried not to see the unflushed toilet in the corner of the cell. He tried to shut off his sense of smell. He tried not to hear the voice of his cell mate. "What 'cha in fa'?"

Without speaking, Elbow walked slowly to the toilet and flushed it.

"Sorry, I wasn't expecting company," the other man's gruff voice sounded truly apologetic.

"Say, what 'cha in fa?"

"They say I robbed a liquor store," was all Elbow offered.

"They do huh," was all the other man said, and he turned his back to Elbow, snuggled his slightly gray head into his uncovered pillow, and said nothing more.

Elbow stood for a long time, staring at the worn mattress that he was to sleep on.

"I swore," he thought. "I swore I would never lay my head on one of these again. I would never have free lodging with the city of Oakland, or any other city, state, or county for that matter." He raised his hand to his face, and wiped the unexpected moisture from his eyes. Giving in to his own

118

weariness, Elbow finally lay on his back. Staring at the dirty gray ceiling, he counted the rain spots and cracks.

"I don't belong here. I don't belong here." These were the only words in his head at the moment. They somehow helped him to keep his mind outside of the cell. It was the only way Elbow knew to get through this.

It was dark in the cell when he awoke. Up and down the cell block he could hear the loud choking snores of the other men. He had slept all evening, after supper, and was wide awake now. Lying there in the dark, Elbow tried not to think of what would happen if he were found guilty of this crime he did not commit. The mere idea of being locked up for more time than he had been already, sent shivers through his body. He closed his eyes tight, trying to chase away the thought.

From nowhere, it seemed, Elbow heard the clinking of keys. He listened in the dark as they came closer and closer.

My bail, he thought. *Bull posted my bail.* Afraid to move for fear he would lose hope, he lay still, holding his breath.

"Ricardo J. Estevan." Elbow hardly recognized his own name.

"Estevan," the voice repeated just as a light was flashed in Elbow's face.

Elbow jolted into a sitting position.

"That's me," he answered.

Again, Elbow heard the clinking of metal on metal. This time, the cell door was being opened.

"Come on." It was a different jailer this time.

"You're free to go," the man announced.

"My bail?" Elbow questioned.

"No, you're free," the man repeated. "There's a guy running around the Bay Area who looks like you. He was brought in just twenty minutes ago. Got caught hitting a mini-mart in Berkeley. Busy fella'. One job a day was not enough for him."

"Just like that?" Elbow questioned Bull, who was waiting to take him home.

"Just like that," Bull answered. "It's disgusting, but it's true. No apologies offered."

"An honest mistake," the guard had pronounced nonchalantly, with no concern in his voice at all.

"An honest mistake," Elbow said, almost sadly. Bull, man, I can't win for losing. I just can't win for losing. What am I suppose to do with that? A night spent behind bars – for nothing. What am I suppose to do with that, man? Huh? What am I suppose to do with that?"

Bull did not answer. He just placed his arm around Elbow's shoulder. The two men walked out of the jail into the balmy, California Bay Area night.

"You in a hurry to get somewhere, Bull?" Elbow spoke after a long silence between the two.

"My time is yours, man. Just say it. What you got in mind?"

"Top-a the Arlington. The city lights would do me some good right now."

"Memories?" Bull questioned quietly.

"Fa' sho'." Elbow became silent, "Christmases," he finally said. "Back when we lived in a two bedroom apartment over on Rheem Avenue. Bull, man, we didn't have much, but my ole' man was a genius...a broke genius, man." Elbow smiled and gazed out of the window.

"That dude could make fun happen outa nothin'." he continued. "Inside a worn out tire swing, or with a dirty piece-a string. Some scraps of wood." Elbow was quiet again. Bull waited.

"But Christmas." Nine children packed in a raggedy ole, beat up Chevy station wagon, up at the top of the Arlington Boulevard, at night. We would ride around the Arlington and look at all the houses decorated from roof to ground. And then. And then the ritual. Pops would park the wagon, and

120

we would just sit. Nobody sayin' nothin'. Just thinkin.' Just dreamin'. Gazin' down on the bright lights all over Richmond, and close-by towns, out across at the Bay Bridge." Elbow paused to think for a second. "I always thought my ole man was try'na figure out a way to get us one of those houses. His dream. We sat lookin' at our Pops dream."

Bull said nothing while his friend took a mental trip back to the best times of his life. He would not dare say a word to interrupt. Bull knew that he had been singled out for a very rare and special moment with Elbow.

"The top-a-the-Arlington," Elbow sighed." Fa'Sho, man, the top-a-the-Arlington".

Without another word, Bull turned the car northbound and drove the long slow route into Richmond, via San Pablo Avenue, until he reached McBryde Avenue. He wanted to give Elbow all the time he needed. The drive seemed to settle his friend.

Locking his attention onto the Lytton Casino to the left, with its high geyser water fountain bright lights, and constant flow of perspective gamblers driving into the parking lot, Elbow muttered something under his breath.

"Say what, man?" Bull glanced sideways at his friend.

"Just wonderin' how this got here," he said, pointing out at the Casino. "Man, talk about outta place in a family kinda town."

"I hear ya, Bow."

Making a right onto McBryde, Bull guided the car all the way up to the top of Arlington Boulevard. Finding a place out of the flow of cars, he parked the vehicle. The lights from the Arlington twinkled all over the city, making one huge yellow glow from as far as the eyes could see. Below them, the city of Richmond sparkled with a brightness and clarity like no other spot in the East Bay. It was a clear night and the Oakland Bay Bridge to San Francisco, visible and friendly, offered its expansive glittering grin to all comers.

"The city." Elbow took a deep breath and let it out. "From up here it all goes away. I can have the power and all the glitter and the shine of the city up here, and not have to put up with all the meanness that goes on down there. I can see them, but they can't spot me. This is what I call peace. Fa' Sho', my ole man knew." The two friends sat for over an hour, talking.

"The mighty Bay Bridge," Elbow suddenly exclaimed, pointing in the direction of San Francisco and the Oakland Bay Bridge." I can almost smell the new, clean, fresh metal from up here." Elbow drew in a deep breath and let it out."

"Funny, ain't it Bull, how quick we throw away old faithful friends."

"What's up with that Elbow?"

"Well, the old bridge. She just sits there now, in the dark. Just a shadow next to the shiny new span, all lit up, leadin' people into the city. Elbow stared out across at what was left of the old bridge. He lowered his head almost as if to offer a moment of silence for what use to be a masterpiece of iron beauty. "And a piece-a-shadow at that," he ended.

"What about it, Bow."

"That old bridge stood there, sturdy and faithful all these years. All kinds of people, from all over the world, comin' and goin', Bull, comin' and goin'. And she carried all of 'em. The stories, man, and the secrets that iron lady must have locked inside-a her."

Elbow moved to the edge of his seat and peered more deliberately out of the front window. "Now, look, just a dingy, dark shadow. Lights out, just sittin' like a long lost friend that nobody really wants to find anyway."

A long moment of silence passed between the two.

"Yeah, I see what you mean,' Bow. But that's life, right."

"That's life," Elbow grunted and fell into silence again.

Suddenly, Bull put the key in the ignition, started the car

and inched away from the curb.

"Whassup,' Man? Guess you gotta run, huh."

"Fa 'sho, dude. Me and you got to listen to some new iron and steel. We got to eavesdrop on some new stories tonight. Maybe tell our own stories."

In the flickering lights of the oncoming vehicles and the semi darkness of the car, Elbow grinned. He mentally drove the car himself, as Bull approached the Bridge from I-80, through Richmond, on through El Cerrito, to Albany, through Berkeley and Emeryville, and then at the fork where Oakland splits in three. Bull steered the Tercel with careful, determined control. Flicking on his right turn signal, he strategically moved the vehicle out of the Oakland and Alameda lanes, to the far right, into a lane which led to the San Francisco, Oakland Bay Bridge.

The white lights of the bridge led them on through the toll stand, where they slowed for Bull to hand a five dollar bill to the agent. The powerful iron arms of the bridge beckoned them. With Bull keeping in time with the 50 mph speed limit, the Tercel accepted the embrace of the massive structure. The two young men seemed to hold their breath under the spell of the new eastern span of the Oakland Bay Bridge.

"273 lights, 23-65 feet high, total of 1,521 light fixtures. Did my homework man. Did my homework." Bull honored Elbow's research with a private grin as he cruised onto the span, letting the soft, icy white lights direct the Tercel onto the greatly illuminated roadway, with its looping cable and soaring tower, majestically suspended in the night.

"The Tercel warmed under the lights, as it negotiated its way into rows of white free-standing light poles lining the skyway deck on both sides. Just ahead of them loomed the 525-foot tower, itself, flooded in light.,

"Light, light, and more light. Man, Elbow, we're riding right into a miracle of metal, steel, and...

"Light," Elbow finished the sentence for him. The two

friends broke out into laughter as Bull steered the car evenly along the roadway entrance to the bridge.

"Takes your breath, huh, Bruh." Elbow gave a soft, low chuckle.

For a moment the two rode in silence. It was Bull who broke the spell of stillness in the car.

"Kinda sad though, Bull muttered, as he turned his head and took a quick look at what was left of the old Bay Bridge to his left. The bridge that had carried millions to and fro now sat like an old used-up iron contraption, as though it never saw a day of beauty or function."

"Sad, he said, more loudly. "There she sits, dark and quiet. like an unappreciated step child. Broken, soon to be forgotten - the old bridge."

"I know, Elbow sighed." "But ain't that just like life. When you got some excitement and fun and useful stuff goin' on, you light up everything around you, and when you're through..." He paused, taking in the length and fullness of the bridge, its heavy, dark, cold steel, stretching in an almost menacing silhouette.

"Well, when you're through, you're through." Elbow blew out a deep breath." They break you up into pieces and leave you just sittin' in the dark."

Gradually returning his attention to the new bridge, Elbow quietly recalled how much he had always loved bridges. He remembered the rides with his family across the many bridges that expanded essential points which connect the nine counties of the Bay Area.

All of a sudden in an exciting Christmas morning voice, he began rattling off the names of the Bridges that connected the Bay Area cities.

"You got the Antioch, the Richmond-Martinez Bridge, the Carquinez Bridge, the Dumbarton Bridge, and the Richmond-San Rafael Bridge. Then there's ya San Mateo Bridge, and the most famous of 'em all, the Golden Gate

Bridge. And Bull, Man, this piece-a work here." For a second Elbow just nodded his head rapidly, as if to agree with himself. "A brutha can feel like somebody again just ridin' 'cross this baby, just being here, Bull, man. No place else in the world like it, Bull, man."

"Fa'sho." Bull grinned at his friend's delight, while expertly navigating the car through the slow lane of the bridge. He had never heard Elbow so excited about anything. For the first time he was seeing the little boy in the young man, and he liked what he saw in his friend. For a minute, neither young man spoke.

It was Elbow who broke the silence.

"And, this is *my* story, homie. This is *my* story. It took some iron and steel, and a flood of lights to make a man untighten his guts again."

"With that, Elbow slid down into his seat, let out a deep breath and rested his head on the back of the cool leather seat."

Bull smiled and said nothing. He was glad that he could be there for his partner. He was glad to be a part of Elbow's moment of peace. Finally, He prepared to take the Treasure Island exit and turn the car around, back to Oakland. Turning the sound up on his GS7, he allowed the music to take them both to a calm and assuring place.

"My man, Kendrick - Kendrick Lamar" Elbow exclaimed! "You got it bruh. fa' sho'! It's gon' be a'ight."

Chapter Thirteen

THE IN-BETWEEN GANG

We're in between a rock and another rock

It was around two weeks after Tailgate and Flippo's night caper, and Elbow's arrest and release. Since it was Tuesday, Bull was off from work. Bright and early that morning, he started out walking to Elbow's. "Some unfinished business," he muttered under his breath.

He continued rehearsing his ideas and going over what he would say to the brothers when he saw them. He had not called them together this morning, but hoped that most of them would be there anyway.

"The party was good. It gave everybody a chance to blow off some steam, but we still gotta talk about this. I got to make the brothers see." The harder his thoughts ran through his mind, the faster Bull walked, until finally, he was unconsciously trotting at a slow, tread-mill pace.

The other's obviously had the same idea as Bull. In fact, they had all arrived ahead of him. MopMan and Cal Q were the first to come bursting through Elbow's door, on the prey for an early morning feed. They both were stuffing down Twinkies from Elbow's pantry. "Breakfast," Elbow had offered, apologizing for the lack of milk to "wash it down."

"Didn't get many hours at the theater this time around. One week up, the next week down. Man can't live on that," Elbow explained. "Funds low. Ya'll cats'll have to feed on your mamas. I'm low."

"We know, man," Tailgate said, pulling open Elbow's cabinet door, and shutting it when he came up empty.

"If we had some organization 'round here." Flippo scowled, throwing a knowing grin at Tailgate, who was still searching for food.

"Besides, you never woulda went to jail for something you didn't do," Flippo continued.

"Leave it alone, Flippo." Elbow shot a hard look at Flippo and held him in place with his I-dare-you stare that he saved for just this type of situation.

"Sorry. My bad." Flippo threw up his hands and backed off.

"I already put that behind me, man. That's how I deal with it. So leave it alone."

"Yo, dawg, I recognize." Flippo stood quiet, stuffing the last handful of Elbow's dry Sugar Crisp into his mouth.

Once again, Flippo opened his mouth to speak, but closed it just as abruptly. Tangling with Elbow when he had that look on his face was like tying yourself up with barbed wire – the first contact drew blood. Cutting his eyes away from Elbow's stare, Flippo accepted his pre-mature defeat and backed farther away from Elbow.

Caught off guard by Elbow's quick reprimand, Flippo knocked into MopMap who held a piece of white bread wrapped around a slice of American cheese, making his way to his favorite corner on the floor. Spinning around and facing Mop, Flippo immediately transferred his defeat with Elbow to MopMan.

"You blind, joker?" Flippo spat out one of his favorite expletives at Mop. "Can't you see I'm in this space? This spot ain't big enough for a real brutha and a wanna-be white boy brutha."

"They call it anger management, Flip." MopMan responded in a calm voice, as he edged around the upset young man. "Do us all a favor. Check yourself into a class, man. You got problems." With that, MopMan seated himself on the floor and began eating his sandwich.

Before Flippo could retort and satisfy his need for a fight, Elbow moved in on him and stood with one hand on Flippo's shoulder and the other extended out toward MopMan, in a steadying gesture.

"Don't have to worry about me, Bow. I told the brutha what I wanted him to know."

"Brutha?" Flippo started, but before he could get the next word out of his mouth, Elbow's deep, daring glare once again silenced him.

Everyone was at Elbow's, even JoJo, in spite of the fact that lately there had been a drastic rise in gang-related crimes in Oakland and his father was keeping a closer eye on the boy. There was a buzz of light-hearted banter in the air as Bull came through the door. Everyone spoke, or gave him a nod or a high-five. There were several jovial comments about the party. It seems that Elbow was right. The party seemed to work to ease some of the tension in the young men. Even yet, everyone seemed in a better mood, except Flippo and Tailgate, that is.

"Hey bruthas, what's up!" Bull greeted them cheerfully as he seated himself on his usual red milk crate.

"You tell us what's up, Bull." Flippo turned his back to Bull, facing Tailgate and began speaking in a low tone to Tailgate.

"What's to tell?" Bull stood and placed one foot on the red crate and propped his right elbow on his raised knee. "What's to tell, Flippo?" We all had a good time....

Before Bull could finish his sentence, Flippo twirled around and pounced at him, positioning himself in Bull's face.

"Good time? Good time? Who had a good time, Bull?" Flippo spat out the words that scorched his tongue. He wanted to burn Bull's face with them. But why spoil it? Why rush in and blow it all up in seconds. It was best to savor the moment, to make the bitter-sweet taste of his spite linger

129

deliciously, like the tartness of the last watermelon flavored Jolly Rancher.

Tailgate moved in behind Flippo. He and Flippo had agreed to take their time as they ripped Bull's ego apart, stitch by stitch, until every seam was torn. They wanted to see Bull there, standing stripped and ruined as their leader.

Both young men placed their hands defiantly behind their backs and rocked on their heels and toes as they faced off with Bull. Slowly and deliberately, Tailgate made his way over to Bull. Elbow, sniffing trouble in the air, moved closer to Bull.

"We got words," Flippo announced, still rocking on his heels.

"Yeah, words," Tailgate echoed. Also rocking.

"Yeah, man, we got su'm to say," Flippo retorted.

"Cool it, men, cool it," Elbow warned, glancing over at Bull.

Good old Elbow. He was always like a kindergarten teacher, warding off play-dough fights. It was Elbow who always carried the peace sign. He just couldn't stand bickering among family and he did all he could to keep it out of The Home. He just wanted the brothers to stick together and remain "cool."

Ignoring Elbow, Flippo jumped back in. "Got a little poem for you, Bull. You like poetry man?"

By now all the others in the room had come around, either standing, squatting, or sitting. They waited to see what Flippo and Tailgate could be so bent out of shape about, especially after the party and all.

"Hey fellas, ya'll like poetry? Raise your hand if you like poetry. Jake, you like poetry. I know you'll just *love* this poem. And it's by a black man too. You love it when the *A-fri-can Ame-ri-can* bruthas write that stuff. Yeah, you'll appreciate this poem." Flippo gave a sarcastic laugh. "Count hands, Gate."

Tailgate was caught up in the mood Flippo had set. All that remorse he had felt when Flippo had run Nicole down concerning Bull, and that second thought he was tempted with when they'd spied on Bull and his new girlfriend - all of it had disappeared. After all, he had no doubt that he would be second in command of The Home soon, and things would be going his and Flippo's way. They figured Elbow would see the light and they would all turn this thing into the real thing. Yeah! This was his moment, and he planned to enjoy every second of it.

"Get on with it, Flip," Bull commanded. "I'll listen to you, but I won't play games with you. But first, Flip, look like a man when you talk to me. Pull up your pants. I told you and everybody in here, that showing your underwear to the world does not make you a man. All it does is..."

Before Bull could finish his sentence, Flippo shot back, "Oh we gon' see who the real man is, Bull. So keep your rules about being a man to yo'self." Flippo was bouncing in place now, hands balled in a fist. He deepened his hot, angry glare at Bull.

Bull raised his voice and shot his fist into the air. "We are men! No one has confiscated our belts, and no one has laid claim to our manhood. Pull up your pants, Tailgate. Pull up your pants, Flippo. Walk like the men you are."

Without realizing his action, Tailgate tugged at his pants from behind.

"What chu' doin' dawg. This dude ain't 'cho daddy." Flippo took his glare off of Bull for a second and threw it hard and mean at Tailgate. Tailgate shuffled nervously and dropped his hands to his side.

Not quite ready to let the subject go, Bull continued. "Think you got swag, Flip. Un un. No way. That ain't swag man. That's drag. That's sag, dude. That's just plain lag. But that ain't nowhere near swag. Walking like a baby with a load in its diaper. Men stand tall, Flip. Men stride with confidence."

Finished, Bull took a deep breath and shot it out in Flippo's direction. "Talk, Flip. You got something more important to say. Talk. But like I said, I won't be playing your games today. You got five minutes to get it out."

"In a hurry, Bull? Nobody stopped you when you got on your swag and sag bandwagon." Sneering and gripping his hands together behind his back, Flippo huffed. "Got somewhere important to go?" Flippo spat out the words, snorting at Bull.

"Okay, Flippo, Tailgate, you called for the floor. Now stop chopin' and get to the point," Elbow ordered.

Elbow's comment was met with an impatient chorus of "yeah, yeah!" Flippo, getting more hyped by the minute, decided it was time to raise the curtain.

"Okay, the poem. Listen carefully Bull. You'll love this."

"A one, a-two, a-one, two, three — da da da, da da dat. Hit it Flip!" Tailgate gave a vaudeville toe-tap and extended his hand in a mock dance sweep. The two voices blending deep and sinister, kept up a rhythm somewhere between a limerick and a rap beat.

> *There was a guy named Bull*
> *who talk all the bull that he could.*
> *His real name was Sherman; let's*
> *shorten it Sherrie,*
> *to match his lover named. . .*

(they paused and shouted at the top of their voices)
CHERI

Without warning, Bull launched at Tailgate and grabbed him by the collar, pushing him back against the wall. "If I ever hear that name fall from your lips again, I'll chip you, Flippo. You too Tailgate. Her name is too good for your mouth. You got that? And my name is Bull to you and everyone else. Understood?"

Bull shoved Tailgate into the wall and grabbed Flippo in his collar, pushing him against Tailgate.

"You got some explainin' to do, and now, lover boy." Tailgate straightened his shirt.

"Sit down, both of ya'll, Now! Bull shouted. "I ought to knock your heads together right here and now," he growled.

Both Flippo and Tailgate knew that Bull was capable of doing just that. They knew he was known for his bull-style fighting. Still fuming, they both sat down on the sunken-seated sofa.

Through it all, JoJo had sat in rigid silence, dark, haunting eyes darting from Bull's face to Tailgate's, then to Flippo's and back to Bull's. He was so mesmerized in the tragic drama unfolding before him that he seemed not to notice the others in the room and they did not seem to notice him. A scowl shadowed his face, when he was not squinting. For a hard second, he glued his eyes to Bull's face and returned to the boys, alternating from Flippo to Tailgate.

Abruptly a tremor moved through JoJo's body and he jerked and then composed himself. He never took his eyes from the two who were causing pain to someone he respected and admired. The worry on JoJo's face grew thicker as he probed Bull's face. JoJo needed to know that Bull was alright.

Suddenly, Jake stood and pointed his finger directly at Flippo, then at Tailgate. As though this abrupt move of Jake was his cue, JoJo jumped up as though he meant to rush Tailgate and Flippo. Squinting nervously at the two, he sat down as abruptly as he had stood. JoJo sat, shaking his legs at a rapid speed, saying nothing. Nothing at all.

Jake spoke, his voice loud, but slow and deliberate. "First, you jokers better understand. a man's gotta be ready to stand and face the one he accuses. Just be ready." Jake let out a deep noisy breath. "You better know what you're doing." Finished, he took his seat.

"I say a brutha's gotta do what a brutha's gotta do," Bop chimed in. He was clearly not on Bull's side at this moment. His face wore that satisfied grin he always gave when he felt that he had really done or said something cool. "And it looks like the bruthas took care of some biz'ness here." His grin grew even wider.

Elbow raised his hand to silence them. Locking the furious two partners into his cutting stare, he took over.

"Talk. You want an audience, you got one. Now talk." Elbow moved in close to the two and spoke directly into their faces. "Talk now or forget it. Just be careful who you try'na punk. That's all I gotta tell ya."

Tailgate gave his speech about Bull's hypocritical ways. He and Flippo revealed how they followed Bull and hid out at the t.v. station. They told the others what they had overheard. Bull listened, controlled, never interrupting. It was as though they were doing him a favor, telling the others what he, himself had not been able to tell them.

Bull was furious, on one hand, that they had the nerve to poke around like two highly paid private eyes, digging into his personal life. On the other hand, he felt a gusty-wind relief, like something in him blowing away, and he could not, nor did he want to stop it.

With his anger and relief, Bull also felt a bit sad that Flippo and Tailgate did not know that what he struggled with the most was how to help them and not let them get hurt. There was no way that the two could have come close to understanding how much the brothers meant to him, and that his secrecy was not malicious as the two pumped it up to be.

But some of the others also failed to understand.

"'Frontin' us, that's all you been doin," Bop screamed at Bull.

This time Elbow was silent. Everyone knew how hotheaded Flippo was, and that Tailgate would follow Flippo wherever. But, Elbow believed instinctively that the two young men were not making this up, at least not all of it. He had suspected that Bull had another life, but he just couldn't put his finger on it. Overwhelmed by the information, Elbow just stood there in his own empty space for a minute, saying nothing.

Elbow waited a few seconds for Bull to deny the story. He had nothing against a brother trying to rise above his circumstances; they all needed to do that. It was the deception that cut to the quick for Elbow. This definitely cast a light of doubt on Bull's interest in the group. For the first time since they had come together, Elbow began to question Bull's loyalty. Was Bull planning to run out on them? What other secrets did he have? And worst, as close as they were, why hadn't Bull trusted him enough to let him in on it?

"That ain't all." Flippo's sneering voice broke through Elbow's thoughts. Flippo would now use the disillusionment showing on Elbow's face to his fullest advantage.

"Yeah," Tailgate added. "You ain't heard nothin' yet."

"Have at it boys. It's your turn. You probably lost a lot of sleep working on this scheme. Have at it." Bull gave a full sweep of his arm and sat down on the milk crate again. Tailgate took a long hard gulp of his victory.

"Well," Flippo went on, "Observe here one well-known woman's man. Lover of all skirt-kind. Here, my bruthas, is the walking Webster on women. See ye him." Flippo made a mockery of eloquence. "See ye him before you – Mr. Playboy, his'self." Flippo stopped to savor the taste of his victory for a second.

"Ya'lll know that mask Jake talks about all the time," Tailgate cut in. "You know, the one in that poem. Say it Jake." Tailgate stopped long enough to throw a taunting grin at Jake. "We wear the mask – huh, Jake?" At this, Jake made a quick move toward Tailgate, but turned back when Bull raised his hand to stop him.

"You sure you brothers want to go on with this?" Jake made an appeal. "Trying to peel off another man's mask can be risky business." He paused, holding his breath suspended in the chilled silence that followed. Exhaling deeply, he let it go.

Cal Q stood against the back wall, his head resting on the sheetrock, his feet wide apart, and his arms folded. On guard, Cal balanced himself for whatever might follow. The muscles of his face were tight with tension, but he did not speak.

"Guess what men," Flippo picked up the drama. "According to one Nicole Jenkins, who did hereby reveal to my partna here, and me. . ." He placed his arm around Tailgate's shoulder. "Did so willingly reveal that in all that time, that one full year, our man, here. . ." He paused and pointed deliberately at Bull. "Our man here never even asked her for it. Mr. Lover Boy here is a . . ." He paused. Both he and Tailgate placed their fingers to their lips, feigning secrecy and spoke in a loud exaggerated whisper. "A VIRGIN!"

A tensed silence filled the room. As soon as it came, the silences erupted into a din of loud talk from some, and a flow of expletives from others. In the confusion that followed, no one noticed that JoJo had slipped out of the house.

Bull did not attempt a defense at this time. He allowed them to hurl their questions and insults, along with their accusations, at him. It was Cal who finally broke into the chaos.

"You wrong man. Both of ya'll – Flippo, Tailgate – you stepped way outta line. You never shoulda…"

"Bull, man, is all this true," Elbow interrupted Cal. Bull and Elbow locked their eyes fast and hard on each other.

"Bull, man, I asked you if this is true? If it is, why the secrecy, Bull? You kept secrets from me, man? Talk to me, partna.' Tell me what's up here." With that, Elbow became quiet, keeping his eyes glued on Bull. The expression on his face was something between hurt and anger.

Abruptly, Bull raised his hand to quieten the brothers. If from nothing but habit, they quieted. "Believe what you want to believe about me. And the truth is. . ." he paused as he stood to face them. "As ugly as they were about it, and as mean as they meant it to be, Flippo and Tailgate told you what I didn't have the nerve to say myself."

He returned his attention to Elbow as he spoke.

"I didn't know how to make you understand, man. I couldn't understand it myself, Elbow. It's like a fight was going on inside me, Bow."

Bull released Elbow and let his eyes move from first one, then the other of them. Jake stood, took one pace in Bull's direction and turned back to his seat. Jake wanted to help his leader out of this mess, but he knew that Bull had to handle his business all by himself.

"Ya'll wanted everything I used to have. I want you to have something better," Bull went on. At this point his hands were stretched out to them, and as he spoke he gestured in honest sincerity.

"Forget 'chu, man," Bop shouted, waving his hand in disgust at Bull. Forget 'chu!" Bop slammed his fist through the air, but he dared not approach Bull. Bop was not really a fighter.

MopMan was still sitting on the floor in the corner of the room with his legs stretched out in front of him. Being a close observer, he usually chose this spot out of the hub of things. He shifted his position slightly, took a panoramic view of his brothers and settled his back into the wall. His face suggested tension, but he said nothing. It was more like Mop to see just where this was going.

Ignoring the constant undertone mumblings of Bop and the glares and the huffs and puffs of Flippo and Tailgate, Bull continued his appeal to his homeboys. By now he had stood and positioned himself in the midst of them.

"Equal time bruthas," he almost whispered. "Home style."

Finally, Elbow beckoned them all to sit. They obeyed. The Home code of communication demanded equal hearings.

Flippo made a move to jump up, but Elbow's barbed-wire stare kept him in place.

Before Bull could continue, Jake jumped suddenly to his feet.

"Is it a bad thing? Huh? Is it really bad? Okay, so our man here appreciates the sustahs. So he respects them, in spite of what we always heard about him. So he stood for his own rights. And is this idea of school really a bad one?"

Throwing his hands in the air at them, Jake pleaded Bull's case.

"Maybe, just maybe our man here got something better to teach us, besides street. . ."

"Shut up Jake. Whose side you on anyway?" Flippo shouted.

"Men!" Bull raised his hands for order. Instantly, Elbow stood with his hands in the air to quieten them again. The noise ceased.

"We're not a gang, men. Bull continued. "That's what I want ya"ll to see. See. We're a family. Sure, we're a bit strange to other people. Most of us are school dropouts, and all of us have problems at home, or no real home to speak of but . . ."

Bull pulled in a long, dry breath and let it out again. "But, we're not like most gangs, if you need to use that word. We're in between. Flippo, we're not gang bangin' and shootin' up drugs, but we're not living in happily-ever-after homes either. School is a world none of us likes. If we gotta be a gang, then call us The In- Between Gang, huh?"

Bull paused to let them take it all in.

"I was gonna tell you about my plans as soon as I could figure it out myself."

Flippo had heard about all he could handle. Without a warning, he flew from his chair and began his tornado, wind-storm pacing. Pounding his fist into his hand, he came face-to-face with Bull.

"In Between," he screamed. "What we in between? I tell you, Mr. Answer Man. We in between a rock and another rock. That's what we in between. No- no, better than that. We between a boulder and another boulder." Flippo was flipping out again. "You wanna hear a better one," he shouted, moving closer to Bull's face. How about this - we in between a mountain and another mountain. Huh, Mr. Cop-Out!" With that outburst Flippo swore at Bull and began pacing again.

No one spoke. All eyes were on Bull. They waited for him to blast Flippo.

Quietly, as if in a trance, Bull moved closer to Flippo. Flippo stopped pacing and squared off to Bull, waiting for the rumble. Just as quietly as he had moved toward him, Bull turned and walked away, taking a seat on the milk crate. Flippo moved with a jerk toward the sofa and threw himself down on it.

Elbow stood, focusing on Flippo. "Maybe that's exactly where we sit, ya'll -in between. We could be half way away from nowhere, or it could be half way to somewhere. Mr. Big don't want us in his face. Mr. Little don't want us either. Elbow opened his arms to include them all. "In Between. Try'na be on the way to somewhere, and don't know a thing about how to get there."

Elbow paused. Scanning the beat-up, shabby place he called home, he let his eyes rest on the area where his new Costco mattress laid. "This - this is as far as I got. Our man here..." He dropped his voice and pointed to Bull. Maybe our man had a feelin' right here." Elbow pounded over his heart. "He coulda wanted to help us get to that somewhere. Just maybe he... Elbow let his words fade out, not finishing his sentence.

Relieved at Elbow's comment in support of him, Bull gave his friend a partial smile and nodded his approval.

"Bow's right. Why can't we be halfway to somewhere?"

The young men shifted uneasily. One by one, they each seem to fall into their own thought at Elbow's words. All, that is, but Flippo, who was not about to let the smooth, easy words of Bull or of Elbow, for that matter, steal his victory.

Even Tailgate showed signs of simmering down. Something about what Elbow said seemed to get to him. For a second, the image of a crying and screaming Nicole flashed before his eyes. All of this, mixed with Bull's and Elbow's words made Tailgate know instinctively that he had some real thinking to do. All by himself.

Flippo was still for a moment. His breath heavy and throaty. His eyes roamed the room, resting on each of the young men. When he got to Tailgate, he just shook his head and looked away. He could read Tailgate's face and see on it his friend's change of heart. Without a warning, Flippo sprung at Bull, throwing punches at him and shouting obscenities. Once again, Flippo was out of control.

Chapter Fourteen

A SCARY TURN OF EVENTS

Too full of pain to know that he cried for them all.

In the tussle that followed, Tailgate, puzzled by his new revelation, still made some attempt to help Flippo. He didn't want to leave his buddy alone in this mess, but his heart was no longer in it. Before Tailgate could move from his position on his knees, Elbow grabbed him in a choke hold and held him in place.

The young man did not struggle. In the meantime, Bull had grabbed Flippo in the same hold. Determined not to lose face in front of the others, Flippo fought his way out of Bull's hold. He stooped, crouched to take a wild swing at Bull, when suddenly the door swung open and JoJo jumped in, brandishing a handgun. He aimed it at Flippo. JoJo stood trembling and crying as he held the gun out in front of him, clutching it with both hands. He kept his teary, angry eyes pinned to Flippo.

Bull sprang up from his seat and stood in front of the shaking and weeping young man.

"I'll shoot'em. I'll burn'em both," JoJo cried. His deep penetrating anguish was soaked in sobs. His voice broke into a dozen heartbreaks. "I'll shoot'em," he cried again.

The silent one, Little JoJo. No one ever expected anything like this from him. But right now he had everybody's attention. The troubled boy was going to use every second of it to be sure that Tailgate and Flippo didn't take from him what he needed more than anything. They would not rob him of the security he got from Bull, and the friendship he received from Elbow.

JoJo had a serious tendency toward sullenness and depression. Basically, he was a silent bystander. Everyone knew how much JoJo admired Bull, but none of them had imagined that he had such an intense loyalty toward him.

JoJo's eyes, in their usual squint, shot out hatred and fear, pain and pride, all mingled sadly in his child's face. His unraveling braids, dangling over one eye, added to his crazed, disoriented look. There was a mixture of shock and fear on the faces of the others as they edged away from the shaky, troubled kid holding the hand gun.

"Come on JoJo, give me the gun. We can talk. Come on, man." Bull spoke in an even whisper as he moved easily toward JoJo.

By now Elbow had let Tailgate loose, and Tailgate was up on his knees in a football scrimmage position. He was afraid to stand erect for fear that JoJo might notice him and give him the bullet aimed at Flippo.

Flippo managed to ease into a standing position, with his hands dropped to his side, mouth open. His eyes were bucked, wide open. He was too frightened to even blink.

"Give Bull the gun, Lil Man. Come on. It's alright," Elbow begged softly. JoJo did not respond; he just stood there trembling and crying, holding the gun, pointed first at Flippo, then at Tailgate. Aiming the gun directly at Flippo, JoJo cried. He was too young and too full of pain to know that he cried for them all. He cried for his never- there Daddy. He cried for his dead mother. He cried for Bull who needed to be set free from JoJo's own deep-digging needs. JoJo's tears rolled down his face, onto his gun hand, and splashed onto the rusty, torn linoleum. Gun in hand, young JoJo's tears washed them all, scrubbing at their pain.

Suddenly, like a gush of water springing from a broken pipe, JoJo's words spilled out in rushed confusion. "They lied to that girl, Nicole. I over heard them braggin'. They lied. They told her you told lies on her so she said all of that bad stuff about . . . they lied. I heard'em."

JoJo's body gave a full convulsive tremble as he almost dropped the gun. The others gasped fearfully. Before anyone could move toward him, the trembling young man regained control. This time he aimed the gun at Tailgate, still in a half-stand, half-kneel position on the floor.

"They tricked her into tellin' them you never made it with her. They lied. They hurt her too. They lied!"

"It's okay JoJo. We don't need the gun to fix that. I'll talk to her. It's okay." Bull consoled. He moved closer to JoJo.

"No!" JoJo took his aim, pointing the gun at Flippo again. "You a man." He turned and directed his words at the others. "Bull's a man. He's a bigger man than all ya'll put together. He ain't got to prove nothin' to nobody. He tough. He helps all us. You got no right to cap on him. I'll kill you." He turned the gun off Flippo and waved it about, taking in the entire room of scared, sweating young men.

As JoJo placed the gun in front of himself again, Elbow sprang at him from behind and with one quick sweep of his hand, drew JoJo's gun hand up into the air. In the same instant, Bull threw himself at JoJo and pried the gun out of the troubled boy's hand. JoJo broke down in uncontrollable sobbing. He cried with all his strength. Finally becoming weak from his ordeal, he dropped to his knees.

Elbow quietly emptied the gun of six shells. Bull quickly gathered the pain-stricken JoJo up into his arms and pressed his head deep into his chest, allowing the boy to empty his anguish into himself. For a moment no one moved or spoke as Bull rocked the whimpering JoJo like a mother rocking her choleric baby.

Flippo was the first to move. Too stunned to speak, he stood staring down at Bull and JoJo there on the floor.

"It's alright. It's over now." Slowly Bull lifted JoJo to his feet and led him to the sofa. He seated him in the comfort of the sunken seat. JoJo sat, head in his hands. Gradually, his sobs began to subside. He simply whimpered now and then like an injured puppy.

In the silence that followed, JoJo suddenly lifted his head and stood up. Squinting through his tears, he pointed an angry and bewildered finger at Flippo. "I'll git 'chu! I'll git 'chu! I"ll show you. Just watch. I'll git 'chu!" Finished, JoJo flopped back down on the couch. Resting his elbows on his knees, he buried his head deep into his hands.

Elbow sat close to JoJo. He said nothing for a moment. As though coming out of a maze, he suddenly shouted to the others, "Okay, okay. The show is over. You can all leave for now." He stared at Tailgate and Flippo. "Ya'll wanted a show. Is this show enough for ya'll? Is this what you set the stage for?" Emotionally spent, Elbow just stared at the two.

"Now listen, all ya'll." Bull finally raised himself from the floor. Pulling the red milk crate over to himself, he sat in the middle of the group.

"This, here..." He talked slowly and deliberately. "What we just saw...nothing compared to what could happen. I know ya'll don't wanna hear this but if you ever had any trust in me in the past, feel me now," Bull took a deep, long breath and pounded his fist over his heart. "Feel me now," he repeated. Bull spoke slowly, clearly and calmly. He focused his eyes on JoJo who sat staring blank-eyed at him.

"I was wrong. I offered ya'll protection. That was okay. I just didn't know how to deliver it. You see, I shut you out 'cause I didn't know how to let you in. I wanted to real bad. I just didn't know how."

"Ah man, forget the crap. You just lookin' for a way out." Bop spoke, his mixed emotions causing his voice to tremble. "And to think, I really placed you up there, man. A fake. You ain't no real brutha, man. You a liar. You been frontin' us all along. Just 'cause baby boy here broke down, don't . . ."

"Equal time, remember?" Bull held his hand up to hush Bop.

"It's true, lil' brutha," he said directly to JoJo. "It's true. I got myself a sweet, beautiful woman in my corner. Cheri. I got a job too. And yeah, I'm planning on going back to school."

"So you just shine us on, huh?" Bop snapped at Bull. "Just front like you care so much, and all the while nothin' really matters to you but yo' other world – yo' own lil secret world."

A cold silence fell on the group. Flippo, shifting his weight a lot, sighed impatiently. Confidence stirring again, he attempted now to open an assault on JoJo as well as Bull.

"And what about this lil' punk threat'n to kill us, huh? What about that?" Flippo was becoming incensed again. Tailgate stared at JoJo but said nothing. No one responded to Flippo's questions about JoJo and his gun. JoJo's whimpering had stopped and he was almost statue still there on the sofa, with his head down, next to Elbow. All eyes shifted from Flippo to JoJo and back to Bull.

"Men," Bull continued. His voice now raised in a slightly higher pitch, trembled with emotion. He paused to clear his throat and settle himself. When he began to speak again, his voice was steady and even.

"Men, I been trying to show ya'll that we don't have to fight. I been out on those streets. I know what's out there. Gang-banging takes lives. I know. My brother, Kebo..."

At the mention of his brother's name, Bull choked up and sat for a second with his head down. "Well, you all know what happened." Bull looked straight at JoJo, who now focused his eyes in his usual strained squint, directly on Bull's face.

Bull looked away from JoJo to Elbow, and then around the room to all the rest. He wanted so badly for them to hear him and to understand thoroughly how much he wanted to protect them. How hard he had fought inside, torn between his two worlds. Above all he wanted them to know that he did care about them. Bull was open now. There was no stopping him. He could feel the walls coming down, one heavy brick at a time. Hal would have cheered.

Check this," Bull continued. Again, his voice trembled; but he did not try to hide the emotion trapped in it. His tone was urgent.

"Check this, bruthas – about women and sex. Bruthas got a right to wait – okay." He paused, taking in the impatient sighs and body language of Flippo, Tailgate, and Bop. He saw Elbow do a double-take, blinking, as though he were seeing Bull for the first time. He appreciated that Elbow did not interrupt him.

Bull kept at it. "A man ain't a man because of how many women he can make it with. He's not a man because of how many babies he can make. Feel me, homeboys," he urged, lightly pounding his heart with his right fist. "And you don't become a man by the number of hearts you can break either. My own daddy told my brothers and me that the minute he spotted the first fuzz under our chins."

Bull's words rushed out now, and the others, in spite of themselves, were caught up in them. "Our father treated our mother like the Nubian queen she was, and yeah, Nicole was like a queen to me. It just didn't work out between us." His eyes were now on Flippo. "Nicole is a special woman, and for sure, I'll go to her and try to straighten this whole mess up. She'll know the truth."

"Yeah, right," Flippo grunted. No one, not even Tailgate looked at him or responded.

"Bull, you don't have too. . ."

"It's okay, Elbow." Bull calmly lifted his hand toward Elbow. "It's alright. I shoulda done this long ago," he assured his partner.

Flippo grimaced and made another impatient sound in his throat, but said nothing. He knew that Bull was still Bull and that when he had something to say, he would say it all.

Bull was on a roll now. There was no way that he could stop. He tossed more bricks aside and he didn't even feel the sand and glass sifting through his mind any more.

"My next step was gonna be to help the rest of ya'll bruthas to get your thing together. That was gonna be my style of leadership. That was my plan. Education and work. Two weapons we can use to fight the odds against us. The two weapons we threw away. I just moved too slow. I just…"

Suddenly Bull stopped talking. Images of his mother on the sofa after Jay's shooting, drifted before him.

"Promise me, Sherman. Let those gangs go." He heard his mother's words again in his head, and they meant more to him now than ever. "I promise." Bull's own words resounded in his head, settling him and freeing him.

Slowly, Cal Q arose and walked over to Bull and extended his open hand. Bull slapped Cal an easy five. Cal turned, walked back to the opposite side of room and stood. Flippo began pacing the floor, but said nothing. He reached for the door as if to open it, but changed his mind and stood near it, shaking and scowling at Bull.

Tailgate didn't even look up. He seemed lost in his own world. JoJo, quiet and almost peaceful now, sat on the edge of the sofa, looking around at the others. Now and then he would turn and focus on Bull. Elbow stood, looked quietly down at Bull and sat again. He too was lost for words. MopMan, still sitting in his corner, with his legs up in front of him now, connected with Bull's eyes and nodded his head, his long stringy hair hanging partially in his face.

"Each man to his own," MopMan pronounced, holding Bull's gaze. "A man's gotta do what a man believes he's gotta do." With that he lowered his head and didn't move.

"Well, I'ma bounce on up outta here," Bop said in a loud, but uncertain voice. He did his cool drag to the door and looked around, obviously needing a response.

"Chill, Bop! just cool it man. This meeting ain't been pronounced over yet." Elbow spoke calmly but firmly.

Bop opened his mouth to speak, but no words came out. When he tried again, all he said was, "I'm cool, dawg." He stood at the door next to Flippo, who was still shaking and scowling.

Suddenly, Jake began a low and careful recitation of one of his favorite Langston Hughes poems.

I Too Sing America.
I am the darker brother.
They send me to eat in the kitchen
When company comes,
But I laugh, and eat well, and grow strong...

Jake stopped abruptly. His eyes were on Flippo who was now shaking just his right leg and mumbling under his breath. The intensity in Flippo's face warned of an explosion.

"Yeah, right," Flippo shouted. "Tomorrow, I'll be at the table when company comes. Nobody will dare tell me to, eat in the kitchen, then." With a gust of sudden outrage he had continued the poem Jake had started.

Everyone, including Jake, looked at Flippo with surprise. Poetry was the last thing they'd expect from him.

"Yeah, right," Flippo said, ignoring the looks of the others. "Good act, Bull. You pulled one over on these jokers. You got game, Mr. Leader. Fooled everybody."

Flippo pointed a defiant finger at Bull. "Well, this darker brutha ain't takin' it, Bull. And Jake. Naw. Naw. Naw, man. 'Cause I'm tired a eatin' in the kitchen. I ain't fallin' for this." With this outburst, Flippo turned and pulled the door open. Before anyone could respond to him, he rushed through the door and slammed it.

Besides, they'll see how beautiful I am and be ashamed. Jake whispered the ending of the poem. *I, too, am America.*

Tailgate hesitated for a moment, shrugged, and spread his hands in a helpless gesture. Without a word, he opened the door and went out to catch up with Flippo.

Chapter Fifteen

LOOKIN' FOR ACTION

It's All About Me

Tailgate had to run to catch up with his fuming friend.

"I'll fix'em," Flippo was muttering as Tailgate fell in step with him.

"What's on your mind, man?"

"Action!" Flippo turned to glare at Tailgate. "Action, Gate!" Some real action. Not just homies and dumb parties. Yeah. Anybody can get some bright lights and a few beats. Naw, Gate. I'm talkin' 'bout the real thing."

Suddenly changing the subject, Flippo turned and started walking backward. His face was a bundle of rage and revenge. His breath was shallow. "You see that lil' punk pull that gun on us in there. Huh, Tailgate. Huh? What about that. I'll show the mama's baby and everybody else. Last time somebody'll wave a gun at me and walk away."

"Ah, that little jive joker ain't got no play, Flip, man. Probably snuck his daddy's gun out the house. Don't waste your t..."

Flippo didn't even seem to hear Tailgate talking at this point.

"I know who to call on, Gate. Yeah, man. I know who can fix me up."

Flippo stopped dead in his tracks, almost knocking Tailgate off the sidewalk. What Tailgate saw in his friend's eyes sent a cold shiver up his spine. He'd seen anger in Flippo's face many times before, but this was the look of someone who was ready to kill.

"Hold up, bruh. Hold up. We can't go there, Flip." "You can't. I can't."

Flippo's breath was heavy and hot in Tailgate's face. One word to one dawg called Boxer, leader of the Whips. "One word, and I'll be in."

Tailgate froze. "Naw man. Naw! Flip, man, I can't feel ya there."

"Gone soft, Tailgate? Like that eye-squintin', bottle suckin' cry baby with his daddy's gun just now? Is that your style now, Gate?"

"Naw, Flippo, you know better. But we just wanna run The Home, not join the Whips. Remember? Put Bull out. Put Flippo in, with Tailgate as his main man. That's what we said we wanted. Remember?"

"And what, Tailgate? And what after that? Play gang and run around takin' little bruthas' lunch money. Is that as far as you can see, Tailgate? Huh, man? Naw, man, something changed back there just now. Something changed big time, Tailgate."

"Think it over, Flip. That's Bull's old gang. You don't wanna go there, Flip, man.

"You think so, Gate? You think so?" Flippo's glare was even colder and deeper. It made Tailgate want to run as far from him as he could get.

"All that crap Bull tried to stuff down our throats just now. That's my ticket, Tailgate. That's my ticket – our ticket, that is if you still with me, man. That's our ticket in. Wouldn't Boxer be interested in knowing how phony his highly admired ex-member really was?"

Completely forgetting for a minute that Tailgate was still there, Flippo began doing a wild and crazy dance, flinging his arms and kicking his heels together in the air. "Now this is somethin' to party about, Gate. Pulling the covers off Mr. Admired, his'self. Lose that chump. Bury his face in his own mud."

"It won't work, Flippo." Tailgate's somber, low voice made Flippo jolt to a sudden stop. Shaking his fist in Tailgate's face, he spoke in an equally somber voice.

"And why not Mr. Knowledge? Just why not?" Flippo stood in front of Tailgate, arms wide open in a mocking manner. "Why not?"

"It won't matter to Boxer, Flippo. There is nothin' you or anyone else can say to make Boxer turn on Bull. Not after Bull saved Boxer's little brother the way he did that time. Kept little dawg from gittin' the life beat out-a him. Naw, man, forget it."

"Yeah. Yeah, I see it now, Tailgate. You want me to wimp out the way you wimped out back there with Elbow, huh, Gate. I saw you, man. You coulda took, Elbow. You just sat down like a little puppy. I saw you, Gate."

"If you saw me man, you saw that choke hold Elbow had on me. The same kind Bull had on you."

"Forget it, Tailgate." Flippo swore bitterly. "I see it as a weak moment." Flippo brushed it off. He couldn't afford to build this thing up and risk losing Tailgate. He didn't want to go it alone. "Forget it, man. Just let me know. You down with me on the Whips or not?"

Tailgate took up a slow, thoughtful pace, moving out a few feet ahead of Flippo.

He said nothing for a minute. Flippo, sensing the urgency of the moment, remained quiet as he picked up his pace and walked side-by-side with his friend.

"Flippo," Tailgate began. "Man, there ain't nothin' I ever let you down on. You know that. Even when it was crazy, I always had your back."

Flippo said nothing at first. He just nodded his head rapidly, realizing the truth of his friend's words.

"But this is asking for more trouble than either one of us is ready for, Flip. Let me think about it, man. This is the craziest thing you…"

153

Suddenly Flippo pounced on Tailgate, slamming his fist into Tailgate's chest. "Forget you, man. You just like all the rest. Forget you. I don't need you. I don't need them. I don't need nobody."

Stunned by Flippo's sudden attack on him, Tailgate grabbed Flippo by the throat with both hands and shook him. "You gon' do me, man? Huh? You gon' do me? You gon' chip me dude?" Tailgate loosened his grip on Flippo and pushed him aside. Flippo stood shaking with rage, but not coming any closer to Tailgate.

"It's like that now, huh, Flippo. Kick everybody's butt. Even mine, huh?"

Giving Flippo one more hard push, Tailgate turned and stalked away. Kicking a supersized 7-11 plastic cup, he crossed to the other side of the street and never looked back.

"Wait up, Gate, man. I didn't mean…" Realizing that his friend was not coming back, Flippo clenched his fist and lashed out at the air with all his might, almost falling with the impact. "I got this," he mumbled, unconsciously wiping a tear from his eye. "I got this," he screamed! It's me! It's about me. It's all about me." Lowering his voice and slowing his pace, Flippo walked on with his head down. "It's about me," he whimpered.

Unaware of the time, and equally unaware of how long he had walked, Flippo finally found that he had come full circle, back to Elbow's. "Maybe I oughta just take care of that lil' punk with his daddy's gun first," he muttered. Then, then I'll go have me a talk with Boxer."

Standing off to the side of Elbow's place, Flippo noticed that the Tercel that Bull drove was gone. Elbow sometimes let Cal Q use his, now that it was fixed, so it was hard to tell if he was still around. He told himself that he wasn't afraid of the two older members, but he just had had enough of them for one day. It wouldn't matter to him about any of the others. He guessed that JoJo was still inside. If Elbow had to go to work, he would have let JoJo hang around as long as he wanted. Something in him just would not let Flippo forget JoJo and his gun.

"If I don't start protecting myself now, then when? You your own man, Flippo," he mumbled as he slowly walked up to the door. "Just don't want no more trouble today," he thought. The courage to open the door evaded him. He just couldn't go back in there right now. Dazed, he walked back down to the sidewalk, turning to look back at the door.

Flippo was torn. He was too enraged to let go of JoJo and the gun scenario. Yet, another face-off with Elbow… He was trapped inside his own explosion. He needed to finish what JoJo started. He had to be his own man. He couldn't let some gun-pointing cry-baby punk him like that and walk away.

"Looking for me?" The voice behind him sounded soft and hard at the same time. He couldn't be sure. Turning around he saw JoJo, just about three yards away from him, pointing the same gun in his face.

"Surprise!" The boy laughed. No tears this time. JoJo just did his usual squinting.

"Yeah, Elbow and Bull need to learn how to hide guns, huh. But before I take this back to my daddy, I can finally get some good use out of it. Huh, Flippo?"

Flippo froze, locked in fear. He could only stare back at the boy with the gun. JoJo was bouncing in place, laughing and pointing his gun. "Pow!' Pow! Pow!" Every time Flippo would flinch, the boy would only roar with laughter.

"Your time to cry, Flippo. Come on, let me see you cry man. Come on Flippo. Cry!" Moving closer to his prey, still aiming the gun at him, JoJo motioned for Flippo to enter the house.

"It's unlocked. Nobody here but me and you, Flippo." Jabbing the gun into Flippo's back, JoJo forced him through the door, entered himself, and closed the door behind them.

155

"Yeah, you, me, and iron man, here." The crazed boy shook the gun toward Flippo. "Good thing Elbow and Bull don't know nothin' about hidin' a gun, huh, he gave an eerie, low chuckle." Flippo said nothing. He just stood holding his breath, waiting for JoJo to make the next move.

"I'll make this fast." JoJo squinted up at Flippo. "I just want one thing from you, punk. I got things to do so don't take long." JoJo held the gun up higher. "Always did want to see how it felt to fire one-a these babies." Suddenly shaking with an eerie laughter, JoJo pointed the gun at Flippo's head.

"Bull is my leader." Getting worked up at the idea of having Flippo cornered, JoJo stood bouncing in place. Sporadically, he pointed the gun at Flippo's heart, then at his head. JoJo's power over Flippo elated him so, he hopped around in back of Flippo, and quickly poked the gun into Flippo's back, and jumping just as quickly back to face Flippo. Again, he pointed the gun at Flippo's head. Poor Flippo could only stand and hold his breath, hoping for a chance to overtake JoJo and claim the gun. He could not believe that this lil punk was holding a gun on him for the second time, in the same day.

"I-WILL-NEVER-DISRESPECT-MY-LEADER-AGAIN! Say that, Flip. Say it. Put your hand over your heart and pledge allegiance to our leader. DO IT NOW," the boy screamed.

Sweat broke out on Flippo's face. He tried to repeat the words, but his mouth just wouldn't move.

"Can't talk now can you mista wanna-be leader."

Getting a much needed thrill out of Flippo's fear, JoJo became more belligerent. "On your knees, Flip. Get on your knees and say it, big mouth. Scream it like you screamed up in our leaders face." He held the gun close to Flippo's heart until the trembling Flippo dropped heavily to his knees.

JoJo was now beside himself with power. The more Flippo squirmed under the threat of his gun, the more excited JoJo became. Moving closer and pointing the gun at Flippo's head again, JoJo screamed, "Bull is my leader. I will never disrespect my leader again. At the count of three, Flippo. At the count of three!" Bouncing in place, with the gun shaking in his hand, the wild-eyed boy counted. "one… two…"

"Bu..Bull is… Bull…" Before Flippo could get the words out, the door swung open and Elbow walked in, positioned himself easily in front of JoJo and snatched the gun from the boy's hand. Pushing JoJo aside, Elbow glared at Flippo, who was now slowly raising himself up from the floor.

"Fool," Elbow shouted at Flippo. Snapping open the gun chamber, he angrily shook it at Flippo. "You woulda been one dead fool if this gun had been loaded, Flip. One dead. dumb fool."

With more rage than he could contain, Flippo raised himself to full height, shook his fist in JoJo's face and bolted from the house. JoJo just stood, shaking and squinting up at Elbow.

Chapter Sixteen

THREE INCHES IN TIME:
No Real News

Nobody Heard His Pain

Three weeks had passed since the traumatic events at The Home, with JoJo and the gun. Bull had heard only from Jake, JoJo, and Cal. He had made no effort to contact anyone. When he walked out of Elbow's place that morning, he knew that he was no longer Home leader. Just as he knew that, Bull also knew that he would always be a brother to the guys. He would never forget them. He would help them, truly help them in any way he could.

But for now, he was eager to find out what urgent message Cheri had for him. Her text message on his iPhone had unnerved him a bit. She insisted on a "face-to-face" meeting at her house.

But what about her father? Bull had thought. He remembered that morning in Cheri's front yard. He recalled the way Mr. Johnston refused to shake his hand. He heard the words again, "We don't need your kind around here." Mr. Johnston had demanded that he not see his daughter. But today, the urgency in Cheri's message overruled any demands from her Dad.

When Bull arrived at Cheri's he met Cal coming up the walk. Puzzled, they both walked to the door, and Bull rang the bell. Cheri answered quietly. Putting an arm around each, she ushered the young men in with a simple, "hello guys."

When Bull and Cal had taken a seat at the dining room table, where Cheri pointed them, she quietly placed a newspaper in front of Bull. She stood silently behind him, with her hand on Bull's shoulder as he read. Cal leaned over toward the paper, scanning.

The news of the shooting hit Bull hard. There it was, the three-inch clipping, tucked in a corner of the Oakland Post. It simply read, *Member of Oakland Street Gang Dies of Gun Shot Wound.*

As Bull read the next line, both his and Cal's faces froze in disbelief. Seeing their homeboy's name on the page right next to the word, "killed," was not what either of them would have imagined at this moment.

"Poor Flip," Bull said. "He thought they had his back, I bet."

"Yeah," Cal added. "Flip just couldn't accept not being on the streets. Just had to go and try to join the Whips. It says here that it was one of the Whips who took Flip out. Flip probably got caught up in the middle of that split going on between Boxer and DogMan. DogMan always did want to lead the Whips. Wouldn't be the first time if he started some stuff to try to get Boxer kicked out.

Flippo never did have street sense." Bull spoke almost inaudibly. "He only had street feeling and feelings can't keep a brother alive out there."

"Even lil JoJo tried to tell'm the other day when he had Flip at the other end of a gun; two times at that. Even though JoJo didn't know it, all lil dawg was doing was trying to save a big dawg." Cal took a deep breath and pushed the paper away.

"Yeah," Cheri whispered. "Everybody knows now that guns don't talk sense."

The three of them, Bull, Cal and Cheri huddled together over the paper, trying to glean some understanding of it all, from one another.

Cal had stuck with Bull since the morning of what turned out to be the split of The Home. With Cheri's help, the three of them had talked JoJo into listening to his father and had succeeded in getting the youngster to go back to school.

"We won't be far, JoJo," Bull had spoken for all of them. "We got your back, man. But we need you, JoJo. We counting on you to show the rest of us how to get it back together with the book learning thing." Cal had encouraged him.

Without even a hint of his usual squint, JoJo had grinned up at Bull, given a round of hand slaps to each, even to Cheri, and made a promise. "For the Cause," he'd said. "For the Cause," they'd all answered. "For the *real* Cause," Cheri had ended.

MopMan and Bop stayed with Elbow, while Jake was happily reunited with his father, traveling with him on his computer sales trips. In a month, Jake would be leaving for basic training. He had volunteered for the Army, and had placed high in office work. His chances of getting a job in that field were excellent. Jake had heard about the shooting and had been allowed to cut his trip with his Dad short to attend the funeral. As for Tailgate, he had dropped out of sight when Flippo left. Tailgate had not gone back to school, but he had started hanging around his family a bit more.

Cal sat at the kitchen table with his head in his hands, saying nothing for a while. Cherie leaned over Bull's shoulder to read the obituary again.

"Three inches of space," she muttered. "It only takes three inches to fill in the life and death of a troubled young man fallen victim of his society and to his own pain."

"What more," Bull muttered, half dazed. None of them had moved from their places at the table the whole time they had been there "When a person's life takes up as little space as Flippo's, who's gonna bother to waste more space on his death?" He settled into silence.

161

Cheri moved around to sit next to him. Taking his hands gently in both of hers, she nestled close to Bull. "Besides," she said quietly, "no one wants to be reminded of the testimony of the lost. The space has to be small."

"I got to go. I can't put it off no more. I got to go now." Cal spoke suddenly.

"Go where," Bull questioned. "We said we would all stay together."

"Naw. Naw," Cal protested. He stood and stuffed his hands deep into his pocket and sat as quickly as he had gotten up. "Naw, Bull, man, I mean I got to go home. See my mother. Take responsibility. Be a man. I got to stand by my child - by Rhea. You know, man."

Cheri shot a quick look of surprise up at Cal, but said nothing. Bull had not told her of Cal's impending fatherhood.

"Yeah," Bull whispered. Cal's words had sent Bull back to one yet unsettled spot in his mind. He thought of his mother, and a heavy sadness engulfed him. "You're right, Cal. Responsibility."

Slowly and absent-mindedly, Bull folded the newspaper and set it aside. The three young people sat for a very long time, saying nothing, but hearing everything, especially the rage that they had known as Flippo.

Bull broke the silence. "It's like Nicole said that night I went out to apologize for what Flip and Tailgate did. *Flippo is screaming so loud for love that he can't even hear himself.* Another long silence ensued before Cheri spoke. "Profound." I'm so glad you went to her, Sherman. After all the hurt Flip and Tailgate brought to that young woman, she understood. Nicole has a good heart."

"Yeah," Bull agreed. "But I shoulda understood Flip, myself. I shoulda understood exactly what Nicole understood. In fact, Cheri, I shoulda been there for my homeboys. I shoulda listened to..."

162

"Well, if this isn't a cozy sight to behold." Mr. Johnston stood at the front door, still holding his grocery bag, easing his brief case onto the floor. The three had been so caught up in their memories of Flippo, they had not heard Cheri's parents come in.

"Well," he repeated, obviously not pleased at the sight of Bull and Cal Q.

"Honey," Mrs. Johnston's voice carried a note of caution. Her smooth tan face wore a calmness, accented by the warmth and kindness that radiated from it. She was a very pretty woman, seemingly in her mid-forties, It was clear that Cheri got both, her good looks and her sweet manner from her mother. She also got her size from Mrs. Johnston. Both were short and petite, with neat, trimmed figures. Neither could weigh no more than a hundred and thirty pounds.

Mr. Johnston, on the other hand, was a looming, bulky, square-shoulder man of frightening proportions. He stood giant-like over his wife, and had the countenance of a boxer about to throw a punch. Though he was a fairly handsome man, he held an overly serious, grim look on his face and a deep stare in his eyes.

From where Bull and Cal Q stood, Mr. Johnston was definitely not someone they would like to make angry. His deep reddish brown skin tone gave him a rough and rugged look, and he must have been no less than 6 feet, five or six inches in height. He spoke in a voice that boomed like it was bouncing off a hard, rock cave wall, echoing back into Bull's and Cal's heads.

Though he made his livelihood as an accountant for Pacific Bell, he boasted often of his experience as a tight-end for the Raiders when they were first in Oakland. His career in football was short-lived due to a leg injury on the field. For sure, Mr. Johnston was not someone Cal and Bull would want to tangle with.

163

Both Cal and Bull stood when Cheri's parents entered the house. Cal shifted slightly, keeping his eyes directly on the man. Bull took a step forward in the direction of the two.

"Hello Mr. Johnston, Mrs. Johnston," he said.

"Daddy, Mom, you know Sherman Bullins from. . ."

"From the streets," Cheri's father cut in, placing the bag of groceries on the table while holding a deadly stare on Bull one second, and on Cal the next.

"Daddy!" Cheri made an obvious effort to remain calm. She knew her father could not stand the idea of her with Sherman, but she had also determined that the day would come when the two would have to come face to face. She regretted that it had to be like this, especially on such a sad occasion.

"Hello, Sherman." Mrs. Johnston extended her hand to Bull, who took it and gave it a light shake. Somewhere in the back of his mind, Bull briefly saw the image of Beauty and the Beast, another story with which his mother had acquainted him as a boy. He had also seen the animated movie. Cheri's mother was the beauty, and for sure, her father was the beast. Not sure of what to do next, Bull quickly sat down.

"And you young man. I don't believe I know who you are." Cheri's mother extended her hand to Cal, who politely shook it, noting how warm and lovely her hand was. All the while, Cal deliberately avoided eye contact with the man whose stare alone could chew him to bits.

"I'm Cal - Calvin Willis," he managed to speak, and quickly sat down, almost missing his seat. Catching himself, he adjusted his bottom to his chair and glued his eyes to the newspaper. Poor Flippo. Too bad a moment like this had to interrupt their private memorial of him. Even in death, Flippo would be the center of some confusion, without even being the subject of it.

"I know'em . At least this one anyway." Mr. Johnston pointed his long, thick finger in Bull's face. "And this one," he pointed at Cal," whoever he is, he can't be worth a Chucky Cheese token either, hanging out with Mr. Gangbanger here." He pointed again at Bull. This time he moved closer to him, glaring down at the young man.

"Daddy, Bull is not in a gang anymore. I told you this. He has not been involved in any gang at all, in way over a year, and he won't be going back. Why can't you listen to me?"

"No." No young lady. You listen to me." Mr. Johnston hotly turned his attention from Bull and Cal to his daughter. "Your mother and I are not spending good money and time on you, for you to just waste it on some back alley, stray, wanna-be Mr. Bad Boy like this one you got sitting in my own house. And after I told you. . ."

"Dave!" Mrs. Johnston's voice was no longer sweet and gracious. It was low, but firm and intentional. Firm enough to make the beast back down a bit. It was clear that the beauty would reign here.

At the tone of his wife's voice Mr. Johnston lowered his, and just stood looking now at Cheri, and then back at his wife. He held his monstrously large hands in the air, palms out, and waved them in slight surrender.

"Okay, okay, I'll leave it alone for now. Just for now." Nodding his head in a disgusted affirmative, he took a step even closer to Bull, and held him in a threatening gaze. The hot breath of the beast heated Bull's face, as he opened his mouth as though he were going to roar. But Mr. Johnston only took a deep breath, blew it out in Bull's face, gave both boys one more glare, for good measure, and walked thunderously out of the room.

"Mom," why does he insist that Sherman is still in a gang? It's as though he doesn't want to believe people can change."

165

Not responding to her daughter's question, Mrs. Johnston turned her attention to Bull and Cal. "I'm sorry, young men. He's just being a watchful father. He hasn't had time to get to . . ."

"It's alright, Mrs. Johnston," Bull politely cut in. "We get this everywhere we go. Some people just remember the newspaper stories about the death of my brother, Jay."

He paused and looked directly at Cheri who walked over and stood near him, placing her hand in his. Still looking at Cheri, he continued. "She's the reason I'm so determined to shake this reputation. And I won't drag her name through anything bad connected to me. I can promise you that, Mrs. Johnston."

Placing his arm around Cheri's waist, Bull continued. "I would never do anything to hurt your daughter. I. . .I. . ." He stammered as a habitual caution tugged at his mind and that old feeling of sifting sand, with glass, tried to get into his words. But Bull was determined. He knew one thing for sure now, more than anything, and he was not going to let the old fears rob him of it.

"Mrs. Johnston," Bull went on. His voice was clear and certain now. He located that deep and soft spot in Cheri's eyes - that spot in which he felt safe and warm and loved, and spoke into it. Mrs. Johnston, I love your daughter."

Once released, the words flew like gentle doves, straight to Cheri's heart, and her eyes filled instantly with water. She had waited so long to hear Sherman say these words. She knew that he had been afraid of them, but now here in front of her own mother, and in front of his best friend, he was declaring his love for her. She did not want to stop the rushing of her heart.

Noticing the slight, almost undetectable hint of a smile on her mother's face, she knew this was the beginning of something good and strong. She could tell by the unspoken words in her mother's eyes, that deep in that place that women often keep to themselves, and between themselves, her mother knew it also. She could hardly contain her joy as Bull slowly brought her hands to his face and brushed a soft kiss on them.

"Well, if this don't beat all. A regular Kodak moment - a real Oscar presentation, if you ask me. A straight-up, You Tube video special, I'd say." The voice of the beast boomed from the door of the hall way. Mr. Johnston stood with his massive frame resting against the door facing as though he had been there a while. He held a portion of a newspaper in his hand. This, he thrust out toward them.

"Is this the kind of love you offer my daughter, boy?" He demanded of Bull. "Huh? Is this it?" Mr. Johnston moved into the room and took two giant strides over to where his daughter stood, holding Bull's hand. He angrily shoved the paper at her.

"Read it Cheri. Read all about how it could end up for your Romeo one day."

"Daddy, don't," Cheri pleaded with him, still clutching Bull's hand.

"Dave, I thought you agreed to leave this alone - at least for now anyway." Mrs. Johnston walked over to her husband and caught him by the arm.

Ignoring the Beauty, the Beast continued his rage. Reading aloud the three-inch testimony of Flippo's life and death, he obviously enjoyed what appeared to be a victory. Poor Flippo, again he would be at the center of a rage. This time he was the subject of it.

"Dante Lewis, alias, Flippo. . ." Mr. Johnston paused, savoring the moment of I-told-you-so. "Flippo." He spat out the name like it was a mouth full of mud. " I wonder why they called him that." The man snarled, relishing his own sarcasm. Glaring at Bull and Cal, the monster roared. "Seventeen year old gang member is shot and killed by one of his own." Mr. Johnston stopped reading, crumpled the paper and threw it in the direction of Bull. The paper landed on the floor.

"The Whips," Mr. Johnston sneered. Now that name sounds familiar. He looked directly at Bull. "Your gang, ain't it, Mr. Bad. Ah, excuse me - Mr. BULL, that is. That is what they call you out there on the streets is it not. Bull. Flippo. Your names say it all. Trouble!"

Having spat out his hostility on them, Mr. Johnston turned sharply on his heels and walked back toward the door to the hallway. Before the man's huge frame could clear the doorway, Cal stood like a soldier posing to salute a commander. He walked over to where the paper was balled up on the floor and picked it up.

"Mr. Johnston," Cal called after the man. Just as erect and with as much control as he had stood and retrieved the paper, he walked over to Cheri's Father, looming there in the doorway. As Cal looked up into Mr. Johnston's face the tears in his eyes glistened, and everyone saw them, especially Mr. Johnston.

Holding the paper out to the sneering man, Cal spoke quietly, his voice thick with emotion.

"We don't need your report, sir. We already have our paper. We already read about the horrible death of our friend." Cal continued to hold the crumpled paper out. Mr. Johnston stood, taken off guard by the calmness and the polite, quiet manner of the boy he did not even know. He just looked down at the young man who dared show respect for a murdered gang member in the midst of his own hostility. He could only look at Cal. But something about his stare had changed. It did not seem quite as beastly as it had a minute ago. He took a step back, turned and headed back into his bedroom. As he walked, he could hear Cal's voice behind him.

"Mr. Johnston, our friend was not a hard thug. He was only a scared young man tryin' hard, just like we're doing

168

here in your house today. He was only somebody try'na get somebody like you to hear his pain." With Cal's words hanging heavily in the air, Mrs. Johnston turned to Cheri and spoke in a hushed tone, respectful of Cal's homage to Flippo, and the grief of the young men standing there. "Cheri, honey, make your friends comfortable and get them a cold pepsi."

Chapter Seventeen

INTRODUCTION TO A LOST POET

Something in me can't reach; It's just too deep

Three days later, the day of Flippo's funeral, Bull clutched Cheri's hand tightly as they stepped through the grass, leaving the cemetery. JoJo, Cal and Jake were with them.

"The sun is shining. The birds are singing and Flippo is dead. Funny isn't it, the way birds sound in a cemetery," Jake said sadly, the poet in him speaking. Birds in the woods or in an open meadow sound free. Birds outside your window in the morning, sound peaceful, happy. Here in the cemetery the birds have respect for the dead – they sing a sad eulogy. That's the job of the cemetery birds. These birds are singing for Flippo."

"Poor Flippo," JoJo spoke in a whisper. "He didn't have to go. Why didn't he listen to you, Bull? Why didn't he listen to me that day. I know I had a gun, but I just wanted to make him see. Why didn't he listen?"

"Flip couldn't hear JoJo." He just couldn't hear. I guess you just plain stop hearing sometimes, especially when the world makes so much noise in your head as it did in Flip's. It just drowned out the sweet sounds and made the bitter ones even louder in the brother's life.

"There was no one there to absorb his pain," Cheri chimed in. "You guys tried, but each one of you had your own loud noises to deal with. You just couldn't read between Flippo's lines. You just couldn't get to him."

The humming motors of the hearse and the family limo could be heard as they idled at the curb. Since no one came to Flippo's funeral but the homeboys and Flippo's family, there was no long impressive line of cars at Rolling Hills Cemetery that morning. At the soft roar of the engines, Bull looked back and across to the other side of the cemetery. His gaze fell upon the mound of fresh dirt under the burial canopy and moved to rest on Flippo's mother as she was being helped into the limo by the mortuary attendant.

The others followed Bull's eyes. "He waits," Jake said. "The grave digger waits to pour dirt over the final hiding place for a seventeen year old black man who never got a chance to live yet. HE TOO, WAS BEAUTIFUL, AMERICA!" Jake screamed out his anguish and let the wind carry his sentiments to rest over the grave site of his fallen friend. "He too was beautiful – he too – he too." His tears felt like wet salt water burning his face.

Bull's voice was low and sad. "More than anyone, Flippo needed someone to hear his pain."

"That's how come he went crazy so often," Cal concluded. "He just flipped out all over the place at the least little thing that didn't go his way." Cal became silent, thoughtful. "Bull man, do you pray man? I mean do you talk to God?"

Without looking at him, Bull answered quietly, "Yeah man, a whole lot more now than I used to – you know."

"Yeah, me too." Cal whispered almost as though he spoke to no one. "Yeah, me too."

"Me too," JoJo chimed in. I always did."

The five walked in silence heading away from the grave site, with the preacher's praying voice and the piteous loud sobs of Flippo's foster mother echoing in their heads. Each carried the weight of his own separate thoughts, yet they all carried the same.

Suddenly, Bull stopped walking. He looked back in the direction of the family in the limo.

"What is it?" Cheri asked. She and the others stood, waiting for Bull to speak. Without answering, Bull pulled a copy of the funeral program from his pocket and stared at it.

When he spoke the others could barely hear him.

"And we didn't even know he wrote poetry. We didn't really know him, Cheri. We didn't know the beautiful stuff locked inside his anger." His sadness sounded heavy in his voice. "I should-a known."

A single tear fell from Bull's eye onto the paper. Cheri stood close to him with her arms wrapped tightly around his waist. Clearing his voice, he read aloud the poem that Flippo's younger brother had found in Flippo's secret lock box and read at the funeral.

Whirlwinds swirl inside my head
Round and round I go.
Where I stop is anyone's guess
I don't like being in this storm –
I look for the calm.
Somewhere there is a place
Where love and beauty grow
They say it's deep inside of me
But something in me just can't reach –It's too deep. . .
Round and round and round I go . . .

"I...I...Bull held the paper to his face." His voice choked with sobs as he blurted out his pain. "I just wasn't there. Not for Flip. Not for anybody. I just wasn't a good leader." As his tears unleashed themselves, Bull clung to Cheri. Feeling the depth and force of Bull's hurt, Cheri buried her head deep into his shoulder.

"You didn't know, man. Nobody knew," Cal quickly offered. "We just didn't know."

"Some kind of leader I turned out to be." Bull could not grab hold of Cal's words. He couldn't be comforted by them.

Pressing his face into Cheri's hair," Bull took a deep breath and let it out. As he raised his head he seemed to have found a modicum of composure.

"I wanted to save him. He wanted to be in a gang. Flip wanted desperately to be part of a gang. I couldn't do it. My...my brother. Gangs took Jay from us."

Unable now to control his remorse and grief, Bull raised his voice in gut clutching anguish." I tried to save him from this!" He waved his arms in the direction of Flippo's grave. "I wanted to save everybody from this. I just didn't know how. I was too caught up in my own..." Unable to finish, the tormented young man again buried his face in Cheri's hair and allowed himself to be quieted.

"Somewhere in Flip was beauty," Cal interrupted, slipping Flip's poem from Bull's hand and looking it over.

"Flip knew what he had, Bull. He just couldn't get to it," Cal concluded.

Bull raised his head and quietly retrieved the poem from Cal. With a firm, clear voice, he finished reading Flip's poem. "Round and round and round I go..."

"Sad," Cheri spoke. "And all we saw was a dark whirlwind where a black man was suppose to be standing."

"Words," Bull muttered, more settled. "Flippo's words." Once again he recalled the quiet mood he had found Flip in one day when the two of them were at The Home alone. The two had talked quietly about football, honeys, and food. But as quickly as it came, Flippo had extinguished the light with a wave of his hand and an abrupt, "gotta run man," leaving Bull standing, stunned. Bull recalled staring at the copy of one of Jake's poetry magazines on the couch next to where Flippo had been sitting.

"Flip loved poetry," Jake added. But it scared him." Jake swallowed hard. "I know how words can be. They can flow easily out of you, soothing your soul, or they can churn around in your gut, stirring up things you don't want to come out and then they come spilling out all over the place. And everybody sees. You can't hide after that. This last is how it was for Flip. He tried to push the words back down. All it did was make him sick." Jake ended with a deep sigh, shaking his head.

"FLIPPO!" A blood curdling scream suddenly filled the air. "FLIPPO!" It came from the direction of the gate that the five were about to approach. They looked up just in time to see Tailgate staggering toward them, raising an opened bottle of beer above his head. Tailgate was dressed in faded light blue jeans and a black Tupac Shakur t-shirt. His black wind breaker swung open as he swayed and swaggered toward them.

"Flippo man. . . I'll get-em. I'll get' em man. . . If it's the last thing I do." Tailgate fell in the grass, got up and staggered in the direction of Flippo's grave, swearing to get revenge on his friend's killers.

As Tailgate neared the spot where Bull and the others stood, Bull and Cal reached for him at the same time, but the young man slapped them both away.

"You did this to him," Tailgate screamed in Bull's face. "You chased him away. You did this to him."

Again, Bull, Cal and this time Jake all reached to help Tailgate. This time Tailgate swung the bottle at Bull, spilling the beer on himself. Swinging wildly, he fought the three and broke away. "You killed him, Bull. You killed poor Flip." Crying uncontrollably he staggered on toward the fresh grave.

"I'll go with you. We'll all go with you, Gate. We'll go to say good-by to Flip." Keeping pace with their friend, Bull and the others, reached a third time for the screaming, fighting Tailgate.

175

"No! Keep away from me. You're the reason he's here. No!" Tailgate would not be consoled. "NO!" Consumed by his own anguish, Tailgate slumped to his knees with his head toward the ground, and the bottle of beer spilling out onto the ground.

Quickly Jake ran to one side of Tailgate, while Bull rushed him from the other side. The two forced their weight under Tailgate's arms and lifted him from the ground. They half dragged, half walked Tailgate over to the fresh mound of dirt, while Cal Q quietly followed. Dropping heavily to his knees, Tailgate cried deep and hard into the dirt, while his friends knelt protectively close to him. Tailgate's anguish welled up from the pit of his gut, shaking his body in convulsions. Cheri and JoJo joined them at the site and watched in quiet sympathy while Tailgate spent his anguish.

Finally, the young men gathered up their broken and whimpering friend. Balancing him between Jake and Cal, they led Tailgate to Bull's car. When Tailgate was settled in the back seat with Cal, Jake took JoJo to ride with him in his old Chrysler, while Cheri settled in the front passenger seat next to Bull. The two cars advanced toward the road, with Bull leading.

"I did it. I did it. The truth. Bull didn't do it." Tailgate repeated his guilt as he let his body go limp in the back seat of the car. "Not you, Bull. Me. I didn't go with him to the Whips. I didn't stop him either. I did it. I never did stop him; not even when he was wrong." The dam inside of Tailgate broke again and his tears gushed out.

"We all let him down, Gate." Cal's voice was calming. It seemed to speak to Tailgate's pain, for the young man's sobs ceased, and he sat still and quiet with his head resting against the back of the seat.

"I lost my friend, my true homie," Tailgate murmured, as though to himself.

We're all here for you Tailgate," Bull promised. "Just let us be here for you, Gate. We're your friends too." Bull's voice was pleading. "We got to make some plans, all of us. We'll do it together. We'll show them. The In- Between - Gang, if that's what we are – we'll come from between that rock and that other rock, Flip talked about. We're on the way to somewhere good, somewhere beautiful."

"We got your back, Tailgate," Cal added quietly. "We got'chu, man."

Silence prevailed. After a few minutes, Tailgate, his voice low and weak, mumbled something the others couldn't make out."

"Didn't understand you, Gate, Cal urged.

"That girl, Nicole, that time. I can't stop thinkin' 'bout her." Tailgate's remorse was intense. "I didn't want to do that to her, Bull. And I know I was wrong for my part, and in that stuff Flippo and me did to you."

Tailgate's sobs found a new momentum. He covered his face with his hands and allowed himself to be washed with his own tears.

"It's all good, Gate. Nicole and I talked. She knows. Don't worry about me man. I'm good. It's you, Tailgate. It's us now." Bull allowed the silence that ensued to settle into the car.

Slowly, Bull eased the Tercel along the streets, curving in and out, through neighborhoods instead of taking the freeway. He wanted to give them more time with Tailgate before dropping him off at his house. He could see through his rearview that Jake was keeping close distance behind them.

Eventually, Bull made a left turn onto San Pablo Avenue in the small city of San Pablo. Making a right turn at Burger King, onto Lowell Avenue, he finally pulled the car up to the curb in front of the dull greenish gray wood house, where the Lopez family lived. Before Tailgate could open the car door to get out, Bull noticed that a burgundy Acura had squeezed in between Jake and him, and had slowed to a stop. Jake had already pulled over and parked behind the Acura. Seeing the puzzled frown on Bull's face as he peered through the rear view mirror, Cheri looked through the back window.

"Daddy!" She exclaimed in disbelief. "What?"

"Oh boy, not again," Bull winced.

"Maybe he didn't get a big enough piece of us the other day," Cal muttered.

"I'm sorry, guys. I'll get rid of him," Cheri promised.

"No," Bull insisted. "It's my turn. After all, it's me he's really after."

Before Cheri could open the car door to get out, Mr. Johnston had already jumped out of his and had rushed to Bull's opened window. In the meantime Jake and JoJo had jumped out of Jake's car and were heading toward the Tercel and the Acura. Seeing Mr. Johnston at the window, the two instinctively sensed trouble. Making their way to Bull's car, they stopped just behind Mr. Johnston.

"Daddy, why are you following us?" Cheri questioned. "Can't you even respect a funeral?"

"Now, just hold on," Mr. Johnston protested, holding up one hand.

"Mr. Johnston..."

"Now listen, all of you." Mr. Johnston cut off Bull's sentence. "Listen. I tried to catch up to you all at the cemetery. You pulled off just as I was turning onto the road."

Peering into the back seat, Mr. Johnston noticed Tailgate, flushed, clothes rumpled and soiled, leaning with his eyes closed, against the back of the seat. By the look on the man's face, he also noticed the smell of beer, but he said nothing. Instead, his face immediately took on an expression neither of the young people expected.

"Cheri, your mother could help. Being a high school principal in the district, and all." With his eyes glued to

Tailgate, Mr. Johnston continued. "School is important, you know."

None of the young people spoke for a moment. The ball was obviously in Mr. Johnston's court and the others had no idea how he would play it. Still leaning into the car at Bull's window, Mr. Johnston placed his attention directly on Bull. Without a warning, he extended his hand through the window.

"I'm Dave Johnston, Cheri's father," he said. A slight smile tugged at the corners of his mouth. "I hear you have some plans, young man, some plans my daughter believes you can pull off. Maybe one day we can talk about them."

Totally taken off guard, as were all the others, Bull accepted the man's powerful hand and returned the greeting.

"I'm Sherman Bullins, and these are my friends. You met Calvin," he said, pointing at Cal. "Behind you are JoJo, and Jake." At this Mr. Johnston turned slightly and nodded at the two standing there. Both boys nodded, obviously in disbelief at what they were hearing. "And the one in the back, shutting out his pain, is Tail...is Jorge Lopez, sir. We all got some plans. We definitely got some plans," Bull said, not realizing how hard he was pumping Mr. Johnston's hand.

Taking back his hand, Mr. Johnston looked them over as though seeing them all for the first time. Without another word, he turned and walked away from the car, returning to his own.

"That's my daddy. You just met my daddy." Cheri smiled.

Chapter Eighteen

I THINK I CAN - I KNOW I CAN

But this is one that I have to tackle by myself

A week later, Bull and Hal were talking as Hal dressed for work. Bull was also dressing, taking extra time to be sure that everything looked just right. It was the first time in a long time the brothers talked without arguing.

"Well, when?" Hal stopped and looked directly into his brother's face.

"When what?" Bull pretended not to know what Hal was talking about.

"You know," his brother insisted, with a half grin on his face.

"Know what," Bull subtlety teased him.

"You're playing dumb on me lil' brother. When am I going to meet my future sister-in-law? That's what."

"Then why didn't you just say that?"

"Well. . ."

"Will you stop digging wells around me? I feel like I'm gonna fall in."

Both brothers laughed freely.

"Okay, next Sunday. I'll bring Cheri by when I pick her up from the studio." Bull started into the bathroom to comb his hair and stopped abruptly. "But control the interrogation. You know how you can be."

"Yeah, yeah," was all Hal answered.

"How do I look?" Bull inquired as he entered the room again.

"I'll go with you, Sher, if you want me." Hal's voice was serious as he looked at his brother.

"I know," Bull answered. "But this is one that I have to tackle by myself. Thanks anyway, man. But there're some things in life that no one can do for you or help you to accomplish. For me, this is one."

Giving his hair one pat with his hand to smooth down any stubborn strands, Bull stepped calmly out of the door. Just as he reached the sidewalk, he heard his name called from someone about a block up the street, in the opposite direction from where he was going. He turned to find that it was Mack.

"Oh no. what does he want now," Bull muttered, as he halted his steps and waited for Mack.

"Hey Bull, glad I caught you, man." Mack broke into a run and did not lessen his pace until he was in Bull's face. Immediately, Bull could see the serious, grim expression on Mack's face. He had never seen this look before. In fact, he had never heard such a somber Mack either.

"What's up Mack?" he asked cautiously.

Out of breath and in a rapid, almost desperate pace, Mack shot out words that Bull had never expected to hear.

"Kebo, Man."

"What about my brother, Mack."

Mack could not hold back the rush of emotion filling up inside him. When he spoke again, it was as though he were finally releasing pinned up words and feelings. He just let the words drop and fall on Bull's ear as they would.

"I ran, man. I got scared and ran man. I know everybody thought I robbed that 7-11, but believe. . ." Mack struggled to catch his breath. He talked fast and desperately. "I got scared Bull, man. I got so scared, I left Kebo. . ."

Mack could not finish his confession. He was too choked up with tears and emotion.

"Cops came too fast. Shootin' started. Kebo and me ran. I thought he was just behind me. I looked back and Kebo was down. He didn't do nothin', man. He was coming out of the Whips. He didn't steal nothin'. We were just chillin' outside the store and . . ."

At this, Mack just broke down and sobbed.

"Forgive me man. Forgive me, man. Kebo was coming in Bull. I wanted you to know. I wanted your whole family to know. He was innocent, Bull. Kebo was innocent."

Bull could not have described the surge of relief that filled him at that moment. He was not angry with Mack. He had suspected all along, as the word on the street had it, that Mack had run and left Kebo to the cops that night. Now that the truth was out, he could not hate Mack. He was relieved to know that like himself, his older brother had had a change of heart about street and gang life. He had come to his senses, and he hadn't committed another crime. Jay had decided to do what their mother had wanted most.

Holding out his hand to Mack, Bull uttered just one word, "Responsibility." Mack looked hard and long at the brother standing before him. Anyone else might have pulled out a gun and mercilessly shot him down for this confession. But Bull just handed him his hand, and the two young men shook.

"A dear friend of mine once said, 'Responsibility can be a killer sometimes.' You know, Mack. It sure can."

"I was scared, man."

"I know about scared too, Mack."

The two young men stood and talked for a long while. Mack filled Bull in on the details of that night his brother died in the street from a gunshot wound from a cop's gun.

"Responsibility can be a killer," Bull muttered under his breath as Mack turned and walked back in the direction he had come.

Bull approached the Tercel, slowly opened the door, and drove to his intended destination. A half an hour later, He pulled the car into a parking slot at the private mental hospital where his mother lived. This was the moment. He had appreciated Hal's and Cheri's offer to come with him, but this was his responsibility, and he wanted to do it alone. He was learning to make decisions. True, the sand and glass no longer sifted through his mind, but decision making was not something to be learned overnight.

Yes, the warm, tender affection he enjoyed from Cheri was slowly healing the scratches and bruises of a rough road traveled. But this – no one could touch the quiet throbbing ache still left hidden deep inside of him. Sherman knew that this could only be relieved one step at a time, all in the direction of a warm, loving woman emptied inside out by pain, pain far greater than his own.

As he walked up the handicap ramp toward the door, Sherman took a deep breath. He stood for a moment with his eyes closed, letting the picture form. In his mind he saw the colored images on his favorite picture book. The bright red engine beckoned him on.

"I think I can. I think I can . . . No!" Sherman almost shouted. "I know I can! I know I can!"

Looking closer at the picture in his mind, he saw the laughter in his mother's eyes. Laughing at her laughter, Sherman Bullins rang the bell and waited to be buzzed in. Once he was checked in by the receptionist, he began the long walk up the sterile white-walled corridor, following the blue-clad attendant as he led the way to the room where Mrs. Bullins lived.

At the closed door he paused, sniffed the one red rose he had selected for his mother and straightened his tie. "For a Nubian queen," he whispered. "For my *first* Nubian queen." Finally, he walked through the door as the attendant held it open.

www.ingramcontent.com/pod-product-compliance
Lightning Source LLC
Chambersburg PA
CBHW071337290326
41933CB00039B/1186